Bob Marley
Roots, Reggae & Revolution

by
Brian Richardson

a Redwords Revolutionary Portrait

Bob Marley on stage

6|

Contents

Acknowledgements | *5*

Introduction: Legend | *11*

01 Repression and revolt:
    Jamaica's colonial history and the origins of Rastafarianism | *15*
02 Post war development & independence | *24*
03 Marley's early life | *31*
04 Sound systems: Ska – and the evolution of reggae | *34*
05 Bob & the Wailing Wailers | *42*
06 Catching A Fire | *47*
07 Exodus | *56*
08 African independence | *61*
09 Redemption Song – a last testament | *66*
10 Rock Against Racism | *75*
11 Legacy | *86*
    Notes

Appendices | *98*

   i.   Bob Marley selected discography
   ii. Fighting fascism today
   iii Reggae playlist

Bob Marley: Roots, Reggae & Revolution
Published by Redwords December 2015
ISBN: 978 1 910885 06 2
Design and production: Roger Huddle
Printed by The Russell Press
Redwords is linked to Bookmarks: the socialist bookshop
1 Bloomsbury Street London WC1B 3QE
       redwords.org.uk
       bookmarksbookshop.co.uk

Brian Richardson is a long time activist who writes
regularly about politics, culture and sport for various
publications including *Socialist Review*. He has edited
two previous books, *Tell it Like it Is: How Our Schools
Fail Black Children* and *Say it Loud! Marxism and the
Fight Against Racism*. He is a practising barrister who
lives and works in London.

Acknowledgements 9

THIS SMALL BOOK has been something of a labour of love for which I must begin by paying tribute to Redwords commissioning editor Roger Huddle. A decade ago I wrote an article to commemorate the 60th anniversary of Bob Marley's birth. It was as a result of this that Roger encouraged me to expand it and patiently persisted every time I promised but failed to deliver. I'm glad that he did, not only because it gave me a great deal of pleasure. It also provided me with an opportunity to correct at least some of the embarrassing mistakes that appeared in that original piece.

Thanks also to Claire, Dave and Albert for providing the loving and supportive environment in which I converted my thoughts into something more concrete. Liz Wheatley, Christian Høgsbjerg and Hassan Mahamdallie read various drafts of the book and generously offered a number of important and helpful suggestions.

Finally, as this book evoked so many happy memories, I have to dedicate it to my parents Hubert and Evelyn and my sisters Joyce and Sharon and brother Adrian.

Brian Richardson December 2015

Trenchtown

Introduction: Legend

THE TERM 'LEGEND' to describe an extremely famous or notorious person, has become somewhat devalued over time through constant repetition and over use. Screen actors and sports stars are invariably referred to as legends after a mere handful of successful films or promising seasons. Indeed at the dawn of the new millennium an admittedly talented American singer-songwriter John Stephens adopted the surname Legend before he had even released his debut album.

There are few terms that could more aptly describe the great reggae musician Bob Marley however and it is fitting therefore that this single word was chosen as the title for the compilation album that was released in 1984 to commemorate his career. In the space of a just a few years from the early 1970s he took a relatively obscure music form from a small Caribbean island popularised it across the globe and used it to promote the fight against racism and the struggle for 'equal rights and justice'.

From the time of his death right through to today, his image has adorned the walls of successive generations of idealistic young-sters alongside that of other icons who 'lived fast, died young and left beautiful corpses'. For many much of the attraction undoubt-edly lies in the countercultural associations of reggae; smoking spliff, relaxing to the heavy bass laden beat of the music and imaging the supposedly easy paced, less materialistic 'no problem' world of the Rastafarian cult.

For others particularly in the black diaspora his significance was more profound. In today's 24 hour multi-media world an endless stream of material is available at the press of a button. The world of the 1970s was very different. In the UK there were just three TV channels, programmes ended around midnight and blac k faces were rarely seen or voices heard. Where they were it was invariably as villains or in ill-conceived comedies such as *Til Death Do Us Part*, *Love Thy Neighbour* and *Mind Your Language*, or the ludicrous *Black and White Minstrel Show*. Similarly, the primetime radio networks stuck to a rigid mainstream playlist. Therefore black families cherished those people who had made it and who could make us feel proud. On the sporting front there was Muhammad Ali the self-styled 'Greatest' a boxing legend, the all-conquering West Indian cricket team and in the charts there was Stevie Wonder, Diana Ross and the Jackson Five.

And then there was Bob. With his long dreadlocked hair flailing wildly as he danced he looked very different. He sounded very different as well. For one thing, unlike countless artists both before and since, he didn't Americanise his singing voice. It was a revelation to hear him sing in a thick Jamaican accent:

> *Dem belly full but we hungry*
> *A hungry mob is a angry mob*
> *A rain a fall but de dirt it tough*
> *A pot a cook but de food nuh nuff* [1]

It didn't take too long for those of us listening to decipher the meaning of those words and when we did we realised that here was a champion of the oppressed.

Marley was thrillingly fluent on stage but many interviewers struggled to understand his shy, sometimes mumbling patois. This led to speculation that he could not possibly have written songs of such complexity which display an extensive knowledge of scripture and black history. A glance at the credits of many of his songs would appear to confirm this. For example, No Woman, No Cry, one of the most famous Wailers tunes appears to have been written by one Vernon Ford. Kwame Dawes, the author of an excellent book, which explores Marley's songwriting prowess entitled *Bob Marley: Lyrical Genius* suggests that the mystery is explained at least in part by the fact that though Marley did in fact write the songs, he often generously credited friends as a way of promoting and supporting them. Sadly this backfired on him posthumously and has led to decades of bitter wrangling over the considerable fortune that his estate has amassed since his death.

Like those other iconic poster boys and girls, James Dean, Marilyn Monroe, Jimi Hendrix and Che Guevara he was handsome and died young. Unlike them however he did not die a dramatic 'rock and roll' death in a fast car, a drug or drink induced haze or in a hail of bullets, though he was fortunate to escape death after being shot and injured in an act of politically motivated violence in 1976. Instead the beauty of this teetotal vegetarian was ravaged by cancer first diagnosed in 1977. For a few short years before his sudden, tragic death though he captured our attention as his music caught fire, burned brightly and led his followers on a wonderful spiritual journey.

Dawes suggests that the reggae star's 'talent is as inexplicable as the talent of any of the great artists of all time. It is pointless trying to explain it.'.[2] Marley was undoubtedly a wonderful lyricist but the suggestion that he or indeed any artist is simply struck by an unfathomable creative muse is wrong. One of the key claims asserted by the great German philosopher Karl Marx is that whilst human beings may make history, 'they do not make it under self-selected circumstances, but under circumstances existing already, given and transmitted from the past.'[3]

The same is surely true of art and culture. Bob Marley was born and lived during a particular, pivotal and turbulent time in the history of Jamaica and was shaped by these experiences. In this respect, he cannot be marked out from his contemporaries which is, perhaps another reason for the posthumous controversy about the origins of his lyrics. Inevitably there are myths, traditions, stories and figures of speech that characterise societies at particular moments in their development. For example the phrase 'Everyday the bucket goes to the well. One day the bottom will drop out' is a well known and popular Jamaican proverb which prophesies that the truth will eventually be revealed as secrets cannot be kept forever. Marley's songs are littered with such references and hence, he used these very words in his 1973 single I Shot the Sheriff. They also appear almost word for word however in The Ethiopians 1968 hit Everything Crash.

Marley was not averse to using words and riffs that he learnt from others. His genius lay in his ability to take what he learnt, develop it and in so doing, capture, articulate and express a mood and feeling in a way that gave his music a universal and lasting appeal. He still speaks to us today and it is fitting that when a *New York Times* panel were seeking out a video which epitomised the 20th century to preserve in a time capsule they chose the recording of his great 1977 Rainbow Theatre concert. Similarly, his 1977 album Exodus was named album of the century by Time magazine in 1999.

This modest offering is in no way a definitive account of Marley or the music that he played. There are any number of excellent books, articles and films that tell us much about the man. Above all there is his body of work that I would encourage all comers to listen to, dance to and be inspired by. What follows then is simply an attempt to examine the world that made Bob Marley and place in context an artist who did so much to entertain, educate and enlighten.

Notes

1 Them Belly Full (But We Hungry) *Natty Dread* (1974)

2 Dawes, Kwame, *Bob Marley: Lyrical Genius*, Bobcat Books 2007

3 Marx, Karl, *The Eighteenth Brumaire of Louis Bonaparte* 1852

1: *Repression and revolt:* Jamaica's colonial history and the origins of Rastafarianism

ANY SERIOUS ANALYSIS of Marley must begin by acknowledging that he was a deeply committed member of the Rastafarian sect. In his authoritative study of the cult, Leonard Barrett Sr describes Rastafarianism as:

> ...a messianic movement unique to Jamaica. Its members believe that Haile Selassie, former Emperor of Ethiopia, is the Black Messiah who appeared in the flesh for the redemption of all Blacks exiled in the world of white oppressors.[1]

Barrett goes on to suggest that for believers, repatriation to Ethiopia is 'inevitable'. The only issue is when Selassie will issue the necessary declaration for the Exodus. It is, of course this journey that Marley invokes on the title track of his brilliant 1977 album.

On the surface this idolisation of Selassie appears preposterous. By any serious reckoning he was an absolutely hopeless ruler. An Amnesty report described him as someone who 'set an alarming watermark for repression and human rights abuses' someone 'whose prisons bulged with dissidents'.[2] Furthermore, whilst he was happy to bask in a certain amount of adulation, not least on a state visit to Jamaica in 1966 he didn't establish the faith. He was in fact a lifelong member of the Ethiopian Orthodox Christian Church. Finally of course, he died in 1975 without issuing any declaration to his supposed followers. Given all of this, one might have expected the cult to die with him. In order to understand why it didn't it is necessary to examine in some detail the history of Jamaica in the centuries which preceded the development of Rastafarianism.

Most official histories suggest that this island of 4,243 square miles located 90 miles south of Cuba was 'discovered' by Christopher Columbus in 1494. In reality a native population known as the Arawak inhabited the land long before Columbus's arrival. It was taken over by Spain in 1502 and by the time that Britain defeated Spain in 1655, the Arawak had been completely extinguished. Subsequently slaves were imported mainly from the Gold Coast and Nigeria to work the land.

Barrett characterises the early history of Jamaica as, 'one long tale of sad intrigue, human suffering, lawlessness and immoral profit, at the centre of which were the African slaves – the ancestors of present-day Jamaicans.'

The production of sugar was a major source of those profits. Following its rout of Spain, the British imperialists set about exploiting the growing demand for sugar and by the early 19th century Jamaica was producing over 100,000 tonnes, 22 percent of the world's supply. This could only be achieved by the most brutal oppression. Barrett adds that:

Slavery in Jamaica lacked any vestige of humanity. A handful of greedy planters held absolute power over thousands of slaves. Only through violence could such complete domination by a minority be initiated and perpetuated.[3]

Where there was repression however there was also resistance. Most mainstream history books would have us believe that the primary reason why slavery was abolished was because of the sterling efforts of powerful and principled white men such as American President Abraham Lincoln, 'the

Great Emancipator' or the English MP William Wilberforce.

The reality is rather different. Instead of passively accepting their punishment and hoping for someone else to liberate them, the enslaved masses frequently fought back against their captivity. As C.L.R. James, the great Trinidadian Marxist who dedicated his life to unearthing and educating others about black liberation struggles and their interaction with wider historic struggles against exploitation and oppression, once observed, 'The docile Negro is a myth… The only place where negro revolts did not take place was in the pages of capitalist historians.' Instead, he argues: 'The Negro's revolutionary history is rich, inspiring and unknown.'[4] Elsewhere, he famously described West Indians as 'the most rebellious people in history'.[5] The Haitian Revolution of 1791-1804 about which James wrote his masterpiece *The Black Jacobins* and the Cuban Revolution of 1959 are two of the most vivid examples of this.

The Maroons

Many of the slaves imported to Jamaica by the Spanish over time developed an irrepressible determination to fight for their freedom, leading to revolts and the establishment of communities of rebel slaves who had managed to escape from the plantations (slave labour camps) known as the Maroons. The ferocity of their resistance in Jamaica was so great that by 1738 Britain was forced to sign a treaty guaranteeing that 'all hostilities shall cease on both sides forever' and ensuring that 'the said Captain Cudjoe (the leader of the Maroons), the rest of his captains, adherents and men shall be forever hereafter in a perfect state of freedom and liberty.'

Whilst this was a triumph, the acceptance by the Maroons of a small area of land around Trelawny was a terrible concession. It was not the worst of Cudjoe's compromises however. In addition to accepting just 1,500 acres of poor quality land, the Maroons agreed to a number of other clauses which ensured that the role they played in the subsequent history of Jamaica was not only resistance but also treachery and betrayal. Clause 6 required them to 'use their best endeavours to take, kill, suppress, or destroy…all rebels wheresoever they be throughout the island.' Meanwhile Clause 9 stipulated 'That if any negroes shall hereafter run away from their masters or owners…they shall immediately be sent back to the chief magistrate of the next parish where they are taken.'[6]

The free Maroons role then was to act as the slaveholders bounty-hunters and it was a task they undertook with as much ruthlessness as they had deployed in the fight for their own emancipation. An early, appalling example of this was their involvement in the suppression of a courageous six month long slave revolt led by a Coromanti slave named Tacky in 1760. An estimated 400 rebels were tracked down and killed including Tacky himself and a further 500 deported to other British colonies.[7]

Sam Sharpe and the Great Slave Revolt of 1831-32

Brutal though such crackdowns were, they could not completely destroy the desire for freedom among the enslaved masses. Thus in 1831 a mass uprising erupted, led by the charismatic orator Sam Sharpe. This was the largest rebellion in the British Caribbean, involving some 30,000 rebel slaves and engulfing an area of 750 square miles, which saw 14 white overseers killed and 100 plantations burned to the ground (causing an estimated £1.1 million of damage). Born a slave in 1801, Sharpe taught himself to read and eventually became a Baptist deacon. This provided him with a platform from which he encouraged his brethren to challenge the inequities of their masters. Emboldened by his congregation's response he hatched a plan for a peaceful general strike from Christmas 1831 onwards, a key period in the sugar harvesting season. Sharpe's idea met with enthusiasm from the enslaved, who thought that anti-slavery legislation had been passed in the British parliament but was being concealed by their masters, and predictable hostility from the authorities who began mobilising troops and warships. Recognising that the strike might be met with violent repression Sharpe made plans for armed rebellion and, indeed the revolt began with a fire being ignited at the Kensington Estate Great House.

The revolt spread with great speed and even saw the formation of a 'Black Regiment' under a commander known as Colonel Jackson, ensuring it took the well-armed professional troops and militia two weeks to reassert control. As Robin Blackburn notes, 'as was always the case, the repression was far more bloody than the original uprising. Some 200 rebels were killed in the course of suppressing the revolt; a further 312 were executed subsequently.'[8] Sharpe was among them and when sentenced to death he went to the gallows heroically declaring, 'I would rather die upon yonder gallows, than live in slavery.'

His death was not in vain though. The rebellion is widely regarded as a central catalyst for the abolition of slavery across the British Empire in 1833. Today the square in Montego Bay where Sharpe was executed is named after him and in 1975 he was named a Jamaican National Hero.

The Morant Bay Rebellion

The heavily compensated former slaveholders continued to rule however and therefore the abolition of slavery did not bring with it the end of colonial oppression.[9] Further protests were inevitable, the most dramatic of which was the 1865 Morant Bay Rebellion. It was led by another black Baptist preacher Paul Bogle who recruited and drilled a group of volunteers in the parish of St Thomas in the north of the island. On the 7th October they marched to Morant Bay whereupon Bogle entered the courthouse, interrupting the proceedings that were taking place. A fight ensued during which two policemen were apparently 'roughed up'. This led to a warrant being issued for the arrest of Bogle and others.

Instead of hiding Bogle figured that he could spark an uprising. He therefore led some 200 to 300 men and women back into town on the 11th October whereupon they again fought with the local militia. Seven volunteers died in the skirmish but far worse was to follow for the rebels. The British Governor-General Edward John Eyre declared martial law and mobilised the Warwickshire Regiment to crush the uprising. They responded with unrelenting savagery killing 439 people and razing 1,000 homes.

A letter written by 'EB' a Warwickshire corporal highlights the scale of the brutality:

> By theire surprise we slotered all before us; we left neither man or woman or child, but we shot down to the ground...I never see a site like it before as we had taken them prisoners by a hundred a day – we saved them for the next morning for to have some sport with them. We tied them up to a Tree and give them 100 laishes, and afterwards put a shot into their heads, and we taken the king of the rebels and hung to the yard arm of one of the British men-of-war ship.[10]

The 'king rebel' was captured on the 22nd October and executed two days later. In total 354 rebels were subjected to summary justice including, controversially George William Gordon a 'mulatto' landowner and dissident politician. Gordon was almost certainly not involved in the rebellion but he was linked to Bogle via his Native Baptist Church.

Believing that he would receive a fair trial, Gordon handed himself in when he heard that he was a wanted man. He could not have been more wrong. Eyre was determined to rid himself of this irritant and intervened directly to ensure Gordon's conviction and execution.

The nature and scale of the repression and lack of due process caused an outcry in Britain. A number of influential figures including John Stuart Mill, Charles Darwin and Thomas Huxley formed a 'Jamaica Committee' which condemned Eyre and sought have him tried for murder. The Governor's defenders included the likes of Lord Tennyson and Charles Dickens and many of the arguments used in his defence such as the characterisation of Jamaicans as lazy and pestilential have subsequently helped to shape modern racism.

Corporal EB's letter found its way to John Bright and was published in his newspaper the *Morning Star*, adding to the controversy and calls for Eyre to be indicted. His stewardship of the island was cut short but he was welcomed back to Southampton in August 1866 with a public banquet organised by his supporters. It was not all plain sailing however. The 'feast of blood' was picketed by a large working class crowd and the clamour for Eyre to be tried increased. This continued for several years but unfortunately injustice prevailed as he was exonerated in both the criminal and civil courts. His legal expenses were paid by Gladstone's Liberal government and the Conservative administration that followed restored his annual pension.

The failure of the rebellion notwithstanding, Bogle is also an official 'National Hero' in Jamaica today as is Gordon, alongside Sam Sharpe, and Bob Marley and for many years his statue stood outside the courthouse in Morant Bay.[11]

Crown Colony to Independence

It was not until 1962, almost 100 years later that Jamaica finally gained independence. Once again, most mainstream accounts would have us believe that this was a relatively harmonious process. Stuart Baker's 2013 documentary *Mirror to the Soul* pieces together Pathe news footage of the Caribbean over five decades from 1920 to 1972. It includes coverage of Princess Margaret greeting both dignitaries and ordinary folk at the independence ceremony and is accompanied by the newsreel's upbeat original commentary. We are told by the plum voiced narrator that the islanders were delighted to remain part of the Commonwealth and that Margaret's elder sister Elizabeth would still be their Queen.

The reality was somewhat different. Jamaica had been designated a 'Crown colony' after 1865. This supposedly afforded it a greater degree of autonomy but the mass of the population remained subordinate and marginalised. Consequently the new constitutional status could not bring an end to hostilities. Independence was finally, grudgingly granted to Jamaica, as elsewhere because Britain's colonial subjects organised themselves, fought for and demanded it.

Sugar production was still a central feature of the economy and it was in this period that Tate & Lyle a relative newcomer moved onto the island having previously amassed most of its profits from Trinidad.

By 1965 production reached an all-time high when 514,825 tonnes were produced. Few of the proceeds made their way into the pockets of the people who toiled the land however and thereafter sugar's centrality to the economy declined. Since then meanwhile Tate & Lyle has been keen to distance itself from its dark history, refining its image by selling off the sugar plants. The name Tate is now more widely associated with an impressive portfolio of art galleries but it should never be forgotten where their founding benefactor's profits originally came from.

In Jamaica a key moment came in 1938 when labour unrest which had been growing throughout the 1930s across the Caribbean erupted and brought organised workers onto the stage on a mass scale. Tate & Lyle's large site in Westmoreland was the site of the most significant protests with over 1,000 workers fighting for higher pay by the beginning of May. The *Jamaica Gleaner* on 2nd May reported that, 'the old factory on the estate which up to Friday had been grinding canes, is entirely in the hands of the strikers'.

The authorities reacted with their customary barbarity. The correspondent continued:

> I hear rifle firing, followed by shrieks and cries...I can see men on the ground. Some are motionless, others are staggering to and fro or crawling away on their hands and knees. The strike has culminated in stark tragedy. A few minutes later I hear that three are dead, eleven wounded and that the police are making many arrests.[12]

One of those who was arrested was Alexander Bustamante, who had been identified as a leading figure in the unrest. This simply inflamed the situation and helped ensure that strikes continued until the end of June. His cousin, the Oxford educated barrister Norman Manley played a key role both in supporting the struggles and negotiating Bustamante's release.

It was out of these events that two major trade unions, Bustamante's own Industrial Trade Union and the National Workers Union led by Manley were set up. Manley and others swiftly saw the logic of transforming this struggle into a wider political movement and consequently made moves to establish the Peoples National Party (PNP) which was formally launched on the 18th September 1938. Whilst it had obvious links to the trade union movement, its founders were careful to ensure that the PNP was a cross-class organisation, with leading figures drawn from the worlds of accountancy, education and architecture as well as the law. The chosen name, deliberately excluding the word 'labour' was a reflection of this.

Bustamante is believed to have joined the PNP briefly but was unable to play an active role as he was soon imprisoned for his trade union activities. Following his release he set up the rival Jamaican Labour Party (JLP) as a right wing alternative in 1943. Subsequently the two parties would battle it out quite literally in the run up to independence and the decades that followed. Both his arrogance and his very definite political leanings are illustrated by the triumphant words Bustamante used when he defeated Manley and won the election to lead Jamaica to independence in 1962:

> In 1938 when I first started to liberate Jamaica it was a time of great national troubles, and we were greatly in need of help of all kinds. I was offered communist help at the time and refused it, for I have always been against communism.[13]

2. Post war development & independence

THERE WERE A number of other dramatic developments both economically and socially in the post war period. In his magisterial book *Bass Culture*, Lloyd Bradley notes that the recovery of the world economy brought significant changes to the island from beyond its borders. The increased wealth enjoyed by a layer of people meant that they wanted to explore different parts of the world rather than holidaying at home. The sun drenched beaches of Caribbean islands like Jamaica made them ideal destinations.

In order to transport these tourists, aeroplanes needed to be built and hotels erected to accommodate them.

Aluminium became a key component in the building of aeroplanes and its chief mineral component is bauxite. By chance this is something that Jamaica has in abundance. From 1950 onwards then the mining of bauxite became an increasingly important factor in the Jamaican economy, growing from less than 1 percent of the island's Gross Domestic Product at the start of the decade to 9.3 percent by 1960. A decade later this had risen to 15.7 percent. In fact the island was the world's leading producer of bauxite from the 1950s right through to the 1980s.

This dramatic growth was double edged however. The mines were owned by large Canadian and American companies, principally Alcan and Alcoa and consequently, most of the wealth created flowed abroad. Bradley suggests that in the 1950s, the mining industry created 10,000 jobs, but at the same time it displaced an estimated 300,000 people from the countryside.[14]

Similarly with tourism, it was the sun, sand and sea that tourists coveted and thus it was on the coastline that the hotels were built. Consequently this also led to the displacement of a significant number of the native islanders. Many moved abroad, it was mainly Jamaicans who first boarded the *Empire Windrush* ship which travelled to Britain in May 1948 heralding the mass emigration of Caribbean islanders to the UK. Contrary to popular perceptions, those that emigrated, whether it was to Britain, the USA or Canada were not the most marginalised. The poorest people could not have afforded the £29 it cost to make that first trip on the Empire Windrush. Instead therefore, the most destitute were forced inland creating ghettoes such as Trenchtown in the capital Kingston.

This bleak history of exploitation, cruelty, betrayal and exclusion was one that Bob Marley was acutely aware of. In So Much Things, also from the Exodus album he implores:

I'll never forget no way, they crucified Jesus Christ
I'll never forget no way, they sold Marcus Garvey for rice
I'll never forget no way, they turned their back on Paul Bogle

And he concludes: 'So don't none of you forget, who you are and where you stand in the struggle.' Elsewhere, there is both an anger and poignancy in his words as he recalls the lies and betrayals of the 'conmen' of colonial era:

Build your penitentiaries
We build your schools
Brainwash education to make us the fools
Hate is your reward for our love
Telling us of your God above

It is for these reasons that his solution is to 'chase those crazy baldheads out of town'.[15]

Marcus Garvey and his influence on Rastafarianism

Given such circumstances it is easier to understand the appeal of Rastafarianism to 20th century Jamaicans especially when one realises how it grew out of the black Nationalist philosophy of the native son Marcus Garvey. He was born in St Ann's Bay on August 17th 1887 a single generation after the Morant Bay Rebellion. In 1914 Garvey founded the Universal Negro Improvement Association (UNIA), an organisation that agitated for equal rights and advocated total separation but left the island just two years later, fetching up briefly in the UK before winding up in the United States in 1916. There he re-established the UNIA, and embarked upon a series of unsuccessful ventures, most notably that of the Black Star Line Shipping enterprise which was intended to provide his people's passage back to Africa. After a spell in prison he was deported back to Jamaica in 1927, but left again shortly afterwards and eventually ended up in Britain where he died in 1940.

Garvey's organisational failures notwithstanding, his importance in the evolution of Rastafarianism is that in a world where racism was so deeply entrenched his promotion of pride and self organisation was captivating. His rallying cry 'Rise Up You Mighty People' is inspirational and it is not surprising that Marley uses it as a refrain on Wake Up and Live, a track on the 1979 album Survival. What elevated Garvey's ideas for those who would go on to establish a new faith was his prophesy that they should 'Look to Africa for the crowning of a black king, he shall be the Redeemer.'

Garvey is believed to have uttered those words in a farewell address before leaving the island in 1916. Thereafter without his charismatic presence his followers were left in disarray, struggling to fuse his philosophy with their own efforts to grapple with the myriad myths, religious ideas and rituals that inhabited the island and which had developed among the masses in the centuries after their arrival.

Ethiopianism and Haile Selassie

1930 proved to be pivotal as that was the year when 38 year old Haile Selassie (known as Ras Tafari) ascended to the throne of Ethiopia and adopted the exalted title 'King of Kings, Lord of Lords, Conquering Lion of the Tribe of Judah'. Ethiopia is a land which is mentioned on numerous occasions in the Bible and for many had attained the mythical status of an African Zion. When Selassie became the new ruler it seemed to many as if he was the embodiment of Garvey's prediction, the Jehovah, Jahweh or to use the shortened term 'Jah', that his followers were looking for. Indeed, initially Garvey himself saw great potential in the new ruler, hailing his coronation and declaring his hope 'that Ras Tafari will live long to carry out his wonderful intentions.'[16] So it was that the cult of Rastafarianism evolved out of this mass of ideas, promoted severally by three main preachers, Leonard Howell, Joseph Hibbert and Archibald Dunkley.

As is now well known, Selassie's internal repression ultimately revealed him as a ruler who betrayed ordinary people but in the middle decades of the 20th century his domestic cruelty was hidden from the outside world. On the international front, despite his diminutive stature, he appeared to be a genuine anti-colonialist leader and champion of the underdog.

He first gained this reputation in the years after Italy's Fascist leader Benito Mussolini launched a barbaric colonial war on Ethiopia in October 1935. Seeking to resist this act of aggression, Selassie broke with precedent, becoming the first Head of State to directly address the League of Nations in June 1936. He delivered a speech in which he sought to 'claim that justice which is due to my people'. The widespread acclaim he received for his anti-colonial stance included being named *Time* magazine's 'Man of the Year' for 1936. It did him little good however. A mere six countries out of the League's membership of 63 opposed Italy's occupation. Selassie was therefore driven out and spent the years from 1937 to 1941 living in Bath, in the South West of England.

Later, many who knew little about the true nature of Selassie's rule were aware of the famous speech he made at the successor United Nations in 1963. It was these eloquent words that Marley quoted verbatim in the song War:

> *Until the philosophy that holds one man superior and another inferior is finally and permanently discredited and abandoned… Until the colour of a man's skin is of no more significance than the colour of his eyes…Everywhere is war.*

The sigh of the oppressed creature

As with Marley's cultural significance the appeal of Rastafarianism must be placed in its historic context and can be understood by reference to Marx's characterisation of religion. It is widely known that Marx described it as 'the opium of the people'. The idea of a drug that dulls the senses, blocking out reality seems particularly appropriate for a cult within which the smoking of marijuana is so central. Marx's analysis was more subtle however and it is worth considering the oft quoted line within the wider passage in which it was written:

> Religious suffering is, at one and the same time, the expression of real suffering and a protest against real suffering. Religion is the sigh of the oppressed creature, the heart of a heartless world, and the soul of soulless conditions. It is the opium of the people.[17]

Rastafarianism's potential appeal is understandable therefore when we consider the concrete circumstances in which it developed. The masses in Jamaica had been suffering for centuries, were struggling to make sense of their predicament and seeking to overcome it. The events in Ethiopia in 1930 and Selassie's subsequent struggle against imperialism seemed to offer hope that this could be achieved in the here and now. Rather than waiting for freedom in the afterlife as so many religions preach, black people were urged to, 'wake up and live'. It is an intoxicating idea and it is not surprising that it appealed to some of those who had previously taken their lead from Garvey.

Attractive though this appeal may seem, in actual fact Rastafarianism was shunned by the overwhelming majority of Jamaicans. It didn't help that Garvey himself, whose ideas remained influential despite his exile and subsequent death later completely revised his original opinion of Selassie, and concluded that, 'It is a pity that a man of the limited intellectual calibre and weak political character like Haile Selassie became Emperor of Abyssinia at so crucial a time in the political history of the world.' He was particularly scathing about Selassie's performance at the League of Nations and suggested that 'Every Negro who is proud of his race must be ashamed of the way in which Haile Selassie surrendered himself to the white wolves of Europe.'[18]

For decades, far from being embraced, Rastafarianism's followers were regarded as the lowest of the low, discriminated against by the island's rulers and driven out of the capital Kingston. It was this victimisation that spurred Howell to buy an old sugar plant in St Catherine's Parish up in the mountains which came to be known as Pinnacle, where he and an estimated 1,600 followers lived a communal self-sufficient existence growing crops, studying, chanting and making music with drums and other improvised instruments. The ritual of smoking marijuana was believed to bring followers into 'oneness' with God as well as having other medicinal benefits.

For the most part, the cult was left to its own devices, isolated and ignored. Every once in a while however its members would be rounded up, roughed up charged and convicted invariably for growing of the illegal 'herb'. Howell himself had a number of spells inside prison.

It was during one of these periods of internal exile that cult followers began growing their hair into dreadlocks and beards. This was a proud and explicit assertion of their African identity in sharp contrast to the trend for straightened hair amongst black people both at home and abroad. It was somewhat double edged of course as it marked them out and helped ensure that they continued to be harassed and bullied when they did descend into the towns and cities.

The Coral Gardens Incident

A particularly notorious example of this harassment occurred over the Easter period at Coral Gardens near Montego Bay in 1963. This was of course less than one year after independence when Marley was a struggling teenage worker. The incident was sparked by a land dispute the previous year during which a Rastafarian, Rudolph Franklin was shot five times and left for dead by a police officer. He survived but was promptly arrested, convicted and imprisoned for possession of marijuana.

Fuelled by a sense of injustice, Franklin returned to the area with a group of supporters following his release. A petrol station was burned down and a bloody clash ensued. Eight people died in the confrontation including Franklin, two fellow Rastafarians, three other citizens and two policemen. Inevitably a major crackdown was ordered by the Prime Minister who was none other than Alexander Bustamante. No longer plain old 'Mr', he had long since bent a suppliant knee to Her Majesty, was now Sir Alexander and is alleged to have declared 'If jail cannot hold the Rastafarians, put them in Bogue Hill cemetery.'[19] On what became known as 'Bad Friday', 150 'beard men' were arrested and jailed. The shaving off of their beards was among the least of the privations they suffered. The following year two Rastafarians, Carlton Bowen and Clinton Larman were convicted of murder and sent to the gallows on the 2nd December.

By the beginning of the 1970s, the plight of the Rastafarians had changed dramatically and this would continue in the years that followed. Demoralisation had set in as independence failed to deliver mass prosperity and increasing numbers of people were looking for alternatives. The percentage of Jamaicans identifying themselves as members of the sect had grown significantly, encouraged no doubt in part by influential figures including Bob Marley who had embraced it.

Michael Manley who had taken over the leadership of the PNP from his father was eager to curry favour in the run up to the 1972 general election and openly courted the cult. He realised that Rastafarians were no longer persona non grata among the masses and he was determined to benefit from this. In a vivid demonstration of the changing times, 100,000 people are estimated to have turned out to greet Selassie when he visited the island in 1966. By the time that Marley died in 1981 the natty dreads provided the most identifiable image of Jamaica and the cult was known about the world over. Barrett estimates that although no accurate record exists, there were around 300,000 followers and a staggering 60 percent of Jamaicans classed themselves as 'Rastas or sympathisers'.[20]

3. Marley's early life

IT WAS INTO this society then, one where the history of slavery and colonial brutality was so immediate, one which was struggling to achieve its independence that Robert Nesta Marley emerged on the 6th February 1945. He was born in the village of Nine Mile, in St Ann Parish up in the north of the island. His comparatively light skin was a consequence of the fact that his parents were a black woman, Cedella Booker and a white British former military man, Norval Marley.

When the Wailers finally achieved international acclaim, the revelation that Bob was in fact of mixed heritage was a wonderful surprise to many casual white followers eager to justify their consumption of weed and explain the decision to grow their hair into dreadlocks. They too could now legitimately claim him as one of their own.

The plain truth though is that this biographical detail encapsulates the contradictions and class divisions of colonial societies. Marley Senior was known locally as 'Captain' though there is no evidence that he was ever anything other than a Private in the British army. What is known however is that he paraded around on a horse and lorded it over his colonial inferiors on the plantations he oversaw. In short, his officer class pretensions were a reflection of the increasingly desperate efforts to maintain British rule in the early decades of the 20th century. It is suggested that Norval genuinely loved and may even have married Cedella. This didn't prevent him from all but abandoning the teenage mother and child within months of Bob's birth. In those early years the family lived in a tiny shack devoid of electricity and Robert spent much of his time tending to cattle, growing crops and chopping wood. This was typical of country life in Jamaica, it was hard and uncompromising.

In his youth, quite understandably, Bob was troubled by the fact that he was a 'half-caste', to use the language of the day. He was treated with suspicion by others in the black community and rejected when he approached Norval's family to assist him.[21] Typically, he reacted to this sleight by writing the song Corner Stone which features on the 1970 Trojan Records album Soul Rebels. As we will discover, like so many Marley songs, it draws very heavily from the Bible. Those familiar with their Christian scripture will recognise and understand the meaning of the phrase 'The stone that the builder refused, shall be the head cornerstone.' As well as appearing at various stages in religious texts, it recurs in

Marley's music, notably in Ride Natty Ride. The fact that there are so many Biblical references in Rastafarianism, and consequently in the music of its followers is a measure of the hybrid nature of the religion.

When Robert was aged 12 Cedella moved the family to Trenchtown in Kingston. She had hoped that life would be easier but arguably it became even tougher and within months she had relocated to the United States leaving her son in the care of relatives. It was here that young Robbie was increasingly exposed to the oppressive violence of the society around him. Police harassment, particularly of the restless youth and those Rastafarians who fetched up in the ghetto was quite simply a daily part of life. It is little wonder then that Marley would go on to write about those who wore 'uniforms of brutality' so vividly in songs such as Crazy Baldheads. Crucially it was during this period that he first met his cousin Bunny and began to play the self-made instruments and learn the folk songs that were such an important part of the island's tradition.

4. Sound systems: Ska – and the evolution of reggae

THE EVOLUTION OF Jamaica's indigenous music is vividly told in Linton Kwesi Johnson's magisterial 10 part radio documentary From Mento to Lovers Rock[22] and Lloyd Bradley's excellent book *Bass Culture*.[23] These studies suggest that up until the end of World War Two, the music that was broadcast into the homes of those people rich enough to own a radio was invariably R&B and jazz recorded and produced in the United States. This continued in the post war period but two key developments heralded a significant change. Firstly, radios became cheaper and more easily available and thus, by the beginning of the 1960s, some 90 percent of households possessed one. Secondly the establishment of the Jamaican Broadcasting Corporation in 1960 created a rivalry with the existing Radio Jamaica Rediffusion which opened up space on the airwaves for new, local music.

For the majority of Jamaicans however the primary source of musical entertainment was provided by the huge and increasingly elaborate sound systems that were rigged up in the streets. There, DJs such as Clement 'Sir Coxsone' Dodd, Duke Reid and Prince Buster engaged in 'clashes', competing with each other to play the most exciting tunes and host the liveliest events. This sound system tradition is one that continues to this day and indeed, is one that has gone on to form a central feature of Caribbean themed gatherings the world over including London's annual Notting Hill Carnival.

| 35

In order to stay ahead the 'selectors' had to source newer, more obscure and more challenging records. Initially this was achieved by sending scouts across to the USA with instructions to find the best available material. Bradley suggests however that:

> Such proximity to the people and the need constantly to reinvent itself at this pace meant that Jamaican music, although based on the American form, would find its own personality sooner or later.[24]

Eventually therefore the DJs moved on from importing records and started to bring together the best local musicians for recording sessions that they themselves had organised. As these records proved popular the logical and lucrative next step was to set up their own studios. The selectors had now become producers and opportunity was knocking for a growing band of musicians. It was out of these developments that the musical forerunner to reggae evolved.

Ska

A number of performers and producers, Dodd, Reid, the guitarist Ernest Ranglin and pianist Theophilus Beckford among them can lay claim to some responsibility for inventing ska. Indeed, Beckford was so bold as to declare that he alone invented it, that 'skavoovie' was the appreciative term coined by the crowds to describe the sounds that he made and that his 1959 release Easy Snappin' is the first ska record. Again, Bradley suggests:

> The black Jamaican tradition is oral, thus scientific precision will be noticeable by its absence. The telling will always be as important as the tale itself, and so it would be going against the general spirit of things to let such a minor detail as factual accuracy stand in the way of a good yarn.[25]

What is not in dispute is that the emergence of ska was the key stepping off point which began the transition from Jamaican musicians mimicking jazz and R&B and instead developing an indigenous sound that would evolve into reggae.

The starting point for this shift was a change in emphasis from the first to the second and fourth (the so called 'off beats') of a traditional four beat bar. In itself this was not the most dramatic of changes, a number of American artists were already moving in that direction. Indeed, it can be heard in its embryonic form on the trademark tune that Dodd's sound system had imported and which he had virtually adopted as his own, Willis Jackson's Later the Gator.[26]

As he began his search for a sound he could genuinely call his own Dodd called a group of musicians led by Ranglin together for a series of sessions. Once assembled they were specifically asked to develop material that placed greater emphasis on this offbeat style. Though the shift was only slight and subtle, it was discernible enough for Ranglin to take the precaution of ensuring that his name was not included on any material that was produced lest it jeopardised the residencies that he had secured in the more conservative clubs and bars.

Another of the key figures who backed these developments was a young man of Jamaican-Lebanese origin Edward Seaga. Born in Boston Massachusetts, Seaga became fascinated by indigenous Kumina folk music whilst conducting postgraduate research as a sociology student. Subsequently he set up the West Indian Recording Limited label (WIRL). Apparently WIRL was one of the few labels that paid its artists a decent rate. Consequently it was a favoured destination for new artists but also and importantly, having been inspired by his earlier studies, Seaga encouraged producers to seek out and record original Jamaican music.

Elsewhere, Bradley notes the contribution that African burru drumming, a central feature of the Rasta commune in Pinnacle contributed to the evolution of the music.

The early Rasta drumming was far more sophisticated than may be supposed, and quickly served to attract Rasta sympathising conventional musicians, playing hookey from the hotel orchestras which resulted in the additions of guitar and brass lines to create a uniquely Jamaican jazz form.[27]

Rocksteady & Rude Boys

The key change that Rocksteady brought about in the mid 60s was a slowing down of the beat. Again, the shift was slight and there was no consciously revolutionary thinking behind the development. On one level, the aim was simply to make it easier for revellers to dance than they could to the more uptempo ska. The gentler beat literally allowed partygoers to 'rock steady' rather than dancing themselves into a sweat soaked frenzy. In turn however it also created space for wider experimentation with bass lines, drumming patterns and the incorporation of the musical influences that had developed over centuries on the island.

As the likes of Linton Linton Kwesi Johnson have argued, notable amongst these traditional forms is what is known as 'Mento', a folk tradition that includes 'call and response' chanting and the use of percussive and woodwind instruments knowledge and the making of which were passed down through the centuries. Such traditions are directly related to Africa therefore and closely associated with the experience of slavery.[28]

Linton Kwesi Johnson also argues that the slowing down of the tempo in rocksteady paralleled the growing sense of despair and hopelessness that began to spread in Jamaica following the initial excitement of the years surrounding independence. Arguably too much can be made of these wider socio-economic developments. Bradley suggests for example that to some extent ska had simply run out of ideas, become too predictable and that 'people just fancied a bit of a change'.[29] He goes on to say that at its heart, 'Rocksteady was the lovers' rock of its time. Celebratory, good time, grab-a-gal music, the soundtrack-to-seduction pop music.'[30]

The Rude Boy phenomenon

Whilst these relatively obvious and simple catalysts cannot be underestimated, like Linton Kwesi Johnson, Bradley also acknowledges a significant if localised social development which was reflected in the music that was coming out of Kingston during those years. There emerged during this period a supposedly restless and lawless group of young men bitter and angry at the lack of opportunity that independence had afforded them. Their lack of respect for others meant that they became known as the Rude Boys.

Unfortunately, but not surprisingly, the Rude Boys solution to their own alienation was not to fight the system but to turn in on their fellow ghetto dwellers. Given that the capital was the focus of the fledgling recording industry and those seeking to breakthrough were often young, hungry and themselves on the edge of poverty it was inevitable that this new development would seep into the music. The life of the Rude Boy therefore became the subject of a number of tracks. The Wailers first single Simmer Down was addressed to their hot-headed brethren and Bob, Bunny and Peter followed this up with a number of similarly themed songs including Rude Boy, Rule Them Rudy, I'm the Toughest and Steppin' Razor. Within a couple of years however the glorification of the Rude Boys by The Wailers and others had been replaced by a growing sense of despair at their antics. Dandy Livingstone's A Message to You Rudy, which was later re-worked by the British band The Specials, to whom we shall return later, began with the lines:

Stop you're running about
It's time you straightened right out
Stop you're running around
Making problems in the town
Rudy, a message to you Rudy[31]

Where Livingstone pleaded with the Rude Boys to 'think of their future' Prince Buster was more forthright. In a series of popular tracks he adopted the persona of the draconian magistrate Judge Dread who rounds up the hooligans, boasts 'I am the rudeboy today' and declares to the wailing youth:

Hush up, hush up!
You're sentenced to four hundred years and five hundred lashes
I'm going to set an example – rude boys don't cry![32]

Few people disagreed with Buster but one who did try to sympathise with the youth was Perry who styled himself as the 'Lord Defender' responding to Judge Dread and argued that the court should Set Them Free.

From Rocksteady to Reggae

Linton Kwesi Johnson identifies 1968 as the key year that marked the transition from rocksteady to reggae, Again however he asserts that it was not a sudden random occurrence and he also claims that its emergence was associated with wider social and economic developments. Selassie's visit and the boost it gave to Rastafarianism was one factor. Meanwhile, as the disillusionment that we have previously noted spread, a fractious general election in 1967 was won by the JLP. Bustamante was replaced by Hugh Shearer, the first black premier. As a local ruling class the government had an interest in promoting nationalism as a way of diverting the masses and was therefore happy to encourage the development of a distinctive Jamaican culture.

A year later the new administration was responsible for a far less positive act which inflamed Jamaican society and must surely have had an influence in the cultural sphere. Guyanese born Walter Rodney was an outstanding student who had gained a first class degree in history on the island at the University of the West Indies (UWI) in 1963. After completing a PhD he returned to teach at UWI in 1968 by which time he was an increasingly prominent advocate of the Black Power Movement and a critic of the betrayals of the ruling elites.

Rodney did not restrict himself to the academy however, he

also gave lectures to workers and the urban poor. Fearful that he had them in his sights and concerned at this grassroots activity, the government responded by banning him from re-entering the country after he left to attend an international conference. This draconian decision led to a series of strikes and riots that highlighted the fact that the new administration would not have things all its own way. Meanwhile, the Rude Boys were growing up to be angry and often armed men with consequences that would turn out to be catastrophic in the years that followed.

Reggae

The ascendancy of rocksteady was relatively short-lived then and Bradley asserts that 'If ska was the birth of modern Jamaican popular music and rocksteady its fairly truculent adolescence, reggae was its coming of age.'[33]

Linton Kwesi Johnson claims that the music that emerged in this period used a strumming pattern which was more similar to that of the old folk songs than during the ska and rocksteady years. Yet this was brought about not by a return to traditional instruments, but, rather, by the creative use of new technology. The electric organ replaced the piano leading to what Linton Kwesi Johnson calls a mento like shuffle pattern. Perhaps more importantly a novel piece of electronic kit called a 'delay' allowed guitarists to develop a new echo sound. The combination of these instruments often amplified by the use of multiple guitars and of course, the ubiquitous drum and electric bass enhanced the effect establishing what finally came to be known as reggae. As ever, the originator of this new music is contested. Coxsone, inevitably, among others lays claim to being its pioneer but again an untold number of people and factors were involved. Rather than a simple and straightforward linear progression from jazz and R&B through ska, and rocksteady to reggae then, it was the gradual fusion of all of them influenced by mento, Kumina, Burru drumming and music from elsewhere in the Caribbean, such as calypso from Trinidad that paved the way for this new music. Added to that a number of factors, the tumultuous march towards Jamaican independence and its troubled aftermath, the establishment of new stations and studios, the increased availability of radios all played their part. These developments created the opportunity for enthusiastic and hungry young artists keen to make their mark and break out of the ghetto.

5. Bob & the Wailing Wailers

THE TEENAGE BOB Marley worked as a welder alongside another enthusiastic young singer called Desmond Dekker who would later go on to be a major international star with songs such as 007 a Rude Boy classic, Israelites and You Can Get It If You Really Want. In 1961 Dekker had auditions with both Dodd and Reid and actually recorded some material for Leslie Kong, though this remained in the vaults for two years before finally appearing in 1963. Nevertheless, his early efforts spurred Marley on to cut his own first disc in 1962 aged 16. The track released on Beverley Records was called Judge Not and offered an early hint of the themes of frustration and oppression that he would go on to address throughout his career. The record was not a success and subsequently Bob was convinced that if he was going to make it, he needed to draw in others. Therefore he recruited Livingston and Macintosh and the group worked together as a vocal trio.

Known as the Wailing Wailers because of their singing style, the group's vocals seemed to capture the anguished cry of alienated youth. They were taken under the wing of the singer Joe Higgs who enjoyed a degree of success himself as part of a duo with Roy Wilson. He was something of a mentor for young artists and more importantly an associate of Dodd. Instead of unleashing the trio immediately though Higgs held them back, made them practice relentlessly and hone their craft. It was worth the wait. When Simmer Down was finally released by Studio One it went to the top of the charts in February 1964.

Despite the success of Simmer Down and a string of other hits in the following years Marley and his fellow Wailers earned little. Jamaican music may have been developing its own increasingly successful sound but while the producers prospered, most artists still struggled to make a living. The session musicians at Dodd's now famous Studio One such as Ranglin and the Skatalites led by the great trombonist Don Drummond were paid a retainer but most were still reliant upon live gigs or other sidelines to make a living wage.

Livingston suggests that the Wailers were paid just £3 per week which was not enough to survive on. Frustrated at this lack of material reward, Bob moved to join his mother in Delaware, Wilmingon in the United States. Whilst there he undertook a range of hard jobs including hotel work and forklift truck driving at car manufacturer Chrysler. The sheer drudgery of this existence is captured in the 1976 Rastaman Vibration album track Nightshift.

On his return to Jamaica, he hooked up again with Bunny and Peter. The Wailers set up their own label 'Wail n Soul n' and sought to challenge the supremacy of the island's 'Big Three'. Soon they were back at the top of the charts with an early version of Bend Down Low. It was also at this point that they began working with Lee 'Scratch' Perry a former junior of

Coxsone's who would go on to be even more famous than his mentor. Heavily influenced by the creative brilliance of this eccentric producer, it was during this period, sometime between 1967 and 1968; a period which we have observed was one of particular tribulation in Jamaican society, that Marley embraced Rastafarianism. From this point on its celebration and promotion was to be the central focus of his work.

Bradley who is clearly a devotee of Perry is forthright in his assessment that:

The work that Peter, Bob and Bunny did with Lee Perry isn't merely the best work that they did as a group, but the best any of them did in any circumstances and that includes all of Bob's later material.[34]

This is a bold assertion with which many will disagree. Regardless, Bradley is undoubtedly right in his assessment of two things. Firstly in strictly musical terms the output is more closely aligned to the pure roots of Jamaican music than Marley's rock influenced output from 1973 onwards. Secondly it was in this period that his new found spiritual beliefs took over and shaped his lyrical content. In short it was here that Marley truly developed his roots rebel sound.

The period during which Marley wrote these songs must have been both frustrating and bemusing but ultimately Bradley argues, the experiences he went through and influences he was exposed to stood him in good stead. He was managed by Danny Sims an African-American who, amongst other things, had been Malcolm X's agent during an extraordinary period of black struggle in the United States which is worth recalling briefly.

The Civil Rights Movement reached its pinnacle in August 1963 with the magnificent March on Washington which concluded with Dr Martin Luther King's famous 'I have a dream' speech. This great movement succeeded in forcing the

Federal Government into passing equal rights legislation but this had not quelled unrest. Instead, the struggle spread from the South to the northern states and evolved into a more militant Black Power Movement. This was epitomised by Sims' client Malcolm who encouraged a fight for liberation 'by any means necessary' and later by the charismatic and equally uncompromising Black Panther Party.

Sims' involvement in that struggle brought the wrath of the authorities down on him and in 1965, the year Malcolm was assassinated, he and his business partner the soul singer Johnny Nash decided to emigrate to Jamaica. It was Nash who first met Bob, was fascinated by the Wailers and invited them to Sims' house. The latter signed them up and gave them enough money to allow some time and space to record.

Between 1968 and 1972 Marley recorded 72 songs and the Wailers released four albums. Nash took some of that material and re-worked it in his own style, scoring a hit with a version of Stir it Up. Crucially therefore Marley came into contact with a singer who could show him what it took to enjoy commercial success but also through Sims he gained a wider political perspective and world outlook. That internationalism was further expanded in 1971 by a fascinating period Bob spent with Nash in Sweden writing and recording the soundtrack to a film *So Much to Believe*. One of the fruits of this sojourn was a wonderful medley of acoustic tracks which were released as part of the 1992 Songs of Freedom box set.

Fascinating though his spiritual and political development must have been and wonderful though Marley's collaboration with Perry was, it did not translate into wider fame and fortune. The four albums he made between 1968 and 1972 netted him barely $200. By contrast, Nash's 1972 album I Can See Clearly Now which included not only Stir It Up but

Publicity shot for Catch a Fire

also Marley's Comma, Comma, Guava Jelly and the joint composition You Poured Sugar on Me sold over a million copies and topped the US Billboard charts. Presumably it was Nash's success that persuaded the white Jewish American actress/singer Barbra Streisand to release a version of Guava Jelly. One wonders whether she even knew what guava jelly was let alone fantasising about spreading it on her lover's belly as Marley's lyrics suggested.

7. Catching a fire

ONE OF THE great ironies of Marley's career is that the catalyst that finally sparked his rise from local notoriety to global stardom was the backing he received not from home based black producer/promoters but from the privileged white Anglo-Jamaican entrepreneur Chris Blackwell. Born in Westminster in 1937 Blackwell had subsequently spent his infancy in Jamaica before being sent to England to ensure that he got a good, solid, traditional public school education.

The origins of his involvement with Rastafarians is the stuff of legend. Bradley reminds us that the 1950s and 60s:

> …was a time when white people's apprehension at the sight of dreadlocks would be almost a given – it wasn't unusual for upper – and middle class Jamaican parents of all races to scare their children with talk of Rasta as the bogey man.[35]

Somewhat improbably having returned to the island of his childhood, the 21 year old Harrow old boy was sailing alone and somehow ended up stranded on a coral reef where he fell unconscious. When he woke up he found himself being tended to for his sunburn and dehydration by a group of dreadlocked fishermen. It was a seminal experience which helped to explode the myths he had learned about the cult. Apparently he vowed that from that day onwards he would do what he could to promote their culture.

Blackwell went on to form Island Records with inheritance money and cash he claims to have earned from scouting work on the first James Bond film *Dr No*. The song that really made his fortune was not released on Island however but on a supplementary label called Trojan Records. Millie Small's *My Boy Lollipop* is not to everybody's taste but is a good example of the sound that was carrying the swing and as Blackwell anticipated it proved to be a huge hit, reaching Number Two in both the UK and US charts.

The success of My Boy Lollipop is indicative of the fact that Jamaican music was developing an appeal beyond its borders. Many of those who had moved abroad longed for the sounds of home, often piling up a sizeable stack of records long before they could afford to buy a stereogram on which to play them. Not surprisingly though Blackwell reckoned that rock music had greater commercial potential. Soon afterwards therefore he sold Trojan Records and turned his hand very successfully to promoting a stable of artists that included The Spencer Davis Group, King Crimson, Traffic and Emerson, Lake & Palmer.

Though he was now based in the UK, Blackwell remained in touch with Jamaica and was aware of the talented and prolific young musician. He was warned against taking the Wailers on however. These ganga smoking Rastas were bad guys he was told, wild, unruly and undoubtedly a waste of money. He thought differently and instead advanced them the £4,000 they requested to make an album. When he later heard the material that the band had recorded he was, to use his own words, 'blown away' by its quality.

That first album for Island Records was Catch a Fire which featured a series of songs that again focused on themes of oppression Slave Driver, Concrete Jungle and 400 Years. It also included a soothing and beautiful version of Stir it Up which was far superior to Nash's effort. Elsewhere, the quirky track Kinky Reggae which features on Side Two has aroused much debate. Its reference to going 'down to Piccadilly Circus' suggests that it is at least in part based upon London. Beyond that, opinion is divided as to whether the song is about the disturbing sight of bizarre sexual encounters or the difficulty of scoring drugs in an unfamiliar location 'a kinky part of town'. Elsewhere there is little doubt about the significance of the 'magic herb'. References to drugs are boldly on display in the album's artwork. The first 20,000 copies of the record were released in a sleeve shaped like a giant Zippo lighter. Subsequent buyers were treated to a startling full face image of Marley drawing on a huge spliff.

By this time, the band had a vast amount of material. Bassist Aston 'Family Man' Barrett reckoned that over time they had recorded a huge number of songs with various different musicians. What appears on the album is work that had been worked on long and hard and finely tuned. Blackwell has often paid tribute to the care with which it was constructed, suggesting that it was the first reggae record conceived of as an album rather than simply a collection of individual tracks.[36] There is nevertheless a distinctly different, arguably less authentically Jamaican sound to it. Despite praising the band's work Blackwell's production included guitar overdubs to give it a rockier sound which he felt it needed to appeal to a wider audience.

With so much to draw on and a hunger to succeed, Catch a

Fire was swiftly followed by Burnin'. The lyrical content is again militant and uncompromising. Burnin' and Lootin' needs little explanation and neither does the unrepentant I Shot the Sheriff. The band were increasingly determined to showcase their spiritual outlook and lifestyle. Rastaman Chant, with its drums very much to the fore is one of the simplest most direct evocations of faith that seems to summon up the spirit of the commune up at Pinnacle.

Small Axe is one of the album's standout tracks and one which vividly highlights both Marley's lyrical brilliance and, again, his deep knowledge of and reliance upon scripture.[37] A version of the song had previously been released on Perry's Upsetter label and, indeed, it should be noted that a dispute about its authorship became a primary source of a protracted dispute between Perry and Island Records. It was re-recorded for Burnin' and includes the central refrain 'If you are a big tree, we are a small axe. Coming to cut you down'.

This is not simply a reference to tree felling. Instead, and in keeping with Marley's identification with the underdog, it stands as a declaration of his determination to stand on the side of the oppressed, encouraging them to come together to take down the high and mighty. In Kevin Macdonald's 2012 documentary *Marley*, Bunny Wailer gleefully explains the origins and not so hidden meaning of these words. Jamaica's pre-eminent producers, Dodd, Reid and Prince Buster had by this time formed something of a cartel which Dodd christened the 'Big Tree' a clever use of patois. Marley's response was a similarly smart play on words. The lyrics were a declaration that his band was one of the 'small acts' that would soon challenge and bring the 'big three's' supremacy to an end. And so it proved.[38]

Having been delighted by the outcome of his first gamble with the loaning of the money to record an album Blackwell knew that the next challenge was to work out how to reap the commercial rewards. For him this meant taking the Wailers out onto the road and promoting them as a black rock band.

This second gamble was initially much less successful in a couple of respects. Firstly Catch a Fire failed to live up to its name, selling somewhere between 14,000 – 24,000 copies in its first year, a paltry figure. More importantly, tensions began to emerge which were to have major repercussions. Bunny was frustrated at the fact that the band wasn't being paid to tour and when the schedule for the American leg was announced he objected to the 'freak clubs' they were expected to play. He told Blackwell that this offended his strict Rastafarian beliefs, refused to travel and expected his comrades to follow suit. He can be seen performing on the London recording that was made for the BBC's showpiece music programme *The Old Grey Whistle Test* but this was to be his final appearance. He left shortly afterwards and was replaced on the tour by the very same Joe Higgs who had begun tutoring the teenage trio a decade earlier.

Tosh hung around until the end of the US tour but he too then departed. He also felt slighted and marginalised by the man he later disparagingly called Chris 'Whitewell'. It was undoubtedly the case that Blackwell saw Bob as the leader and to a great extent as the main songwriter this was true, but it should not be forgotten that both Bunny and Tosh had made a major contribution. It was Tosh for example who wrote one of the band's most militant songs Get Up, Stand Up, the lead track on Burnin'.

From 1974 onwards then Marley was forced to establish a new line up. The Barrett brothers, Carlton and 'Family Man' remained on drum and bass respectively, but they were supplemented over time by a number of others including guitarists, Al Anderson, Donald Kinsey and Junior Marvin.

Tyrone Downie and Earl 'Wya' Lindo played keyboards and Alvin 'Seeco' Patterson came in on percussion. In addition three female backing singers, Marley's wife Rita, Marcia Griffiths and Judy Mowatt collectively known as the I-Threes became a permanent feature of the band from that year on.

Bob's willingness to compromise both in terms of Blackwell's re-shaping of Catch of Fire and the tour schedule highlights an important point not just about him but about culture in general. It isn't created in a vacuum hermetically sealed from all of the influences of wider society. Indeed, the test of great art is surely its ability to connect with people and not simply entertain but also to encourage us to view and think about the world in novel and challenging ways. Artists need to survive however and are therefore rarely completely free to 'express themselves'. Instead, they are invariably subject to the preferences, constraints, deadlines and commercial considerations of their patrons. This was undoubtedly true of Marley. He was prepared to sacrifice Peter and Bunny, a degree of control over his music and arguably, a certain amount of credibility among his 'bredrin' back in JA in his quest for wider recognition. There are some who would criticise him for this but it is is to his credit that he did not tone down his lyrical content.

The Wailers' 1975 London Lyceum Ballroom concert is widely regarded as one of popular music's truly outstanding gigs. Blackwell for one considered it to be the 'tipping point' that really cemented the band's reputation and catapulted Marley to international superstardom. In turn it netted him enough money to purchase and take over Blackwell's sprawling home cum studio at 56 Hope Road in Kingston. His posh neighbours in this most prestigious of streets, including the Prime Minister and Governor-General must have bristled as he and a very merry band of friends and lovers hung out, made love, played football, cooked up huge pots of 'Ital' food, smoked prodigious amounts of ganga and composed some of the most magnificent anti-establishment music the world has ever heard.

'Politricks'

Marley may have found himself living down the road from Government House but he was scathing about the lies and betrayals of those involved in what he called 'politricks'. On Revolution from 1974's Natty Dread he declares 'Never make a politician grant you a favour, they will always want to control you forever'. The song's title clearly highlights his preferred alternative. It is interesting to note though that Michael Manley recalled that the first time he encountered Bob was in 1971 and that for the next 12 months the young musician performed as part of a group of artists who toured the island with the PNP's Musical Bandwagon initiative as the party embarked on a successful campaign which saw Manley elected as prime minister for the first time in 1972.[39]

Ambush in the Night: The Smile Jamaica Concert

In 1976 there came an event that literally scarred the reggae star. It had been a hugely successful year for the Wailers, with that year's album release Rastaman Vibration reaching Number 8 on the Billboard chart. Marley's global status meant that he was now performing alongside the world's biggest artists including Motown megastar Stevie Wonder. Apparently Stevie had donated half of his fee for a 1975 concert performance on the island to a local school for the blind. Bob decided that he too wanted to perform a similar act of charity and therefore announced an intention to put on a free concert for the people of Jamaica. It was scheduled for the 5th December under the banner 'Smile Jamaica'.

Eyeing an opportunity to gain political advantage, Manley latched onto the idea offering to host the event in the grounds of his official residence Jamaica House. Marley insisted that it should be somewhere neutral, so instead it was scheduled for the National Heroes Park at Kingston Racecourse, but it was still billed as an event organised 'by Bob Marley in association with the cultural section of the Prime Minister's Office.' Not wanting to miss his opportunity Manley promptly announced that a general election would be held on the 15th December. This spelled big trouble for Marley. Jamaica was in a mess and for many the blame lay squarely at the feet of Michael Manley.

The demoralisation that had begun to develop in the mid 1960s had long since settled into a deeply entrenched malaise. By the mid 1970s, 80 percent of the island's wealth was still owned by just 2 percent of the population and an estimated 24 percent of adults were unemployed. Manley's supposedly socialist government seemed incapable of solving the problems and he found himself being increasing challenged by the JLP now led by Edward Seaga a man whose political ambitions had long since replaced any interest in promoting local music. Far from leading any sort of genuine workers party, he was widely dubbed 'CIA -ga' as it was well known that he was being backed by the US Secret Service who objected to Manley's flirtations with Russia and Fidel Castro's Cuba. Evidently Seaga was not averse to using covert and undemocratic means to get his way but neither was Manley.

A bitter rivalry had existed between the two parties since the 1940s as they jockeyed for position in the run up to independence. In its aftermath this had escalated and by the 1970s it had exploded into fully fledged sectarian division. The grim reality of corruption, violent patronage and CIA subterfuge is vividly portrayed in Macdonald's documentary *Marley*[40] and Marlon James wonderful novel *A Brief History of Seven Killings*.[41]. Quite simply vast sections of the island were divided into zones controlled by gangs who were armed and paid by the rival parties.

By announcing the concert it appeared therefore as if Marley was making a partisan intervention on behalf of the PNP and thus he was putting his life in peril. Numerous people including Blackwell warned him of the risk but he was determined to press on in the hope that the public would realise that this was a humanitarian not a political act. His generosity nearly cost him his life. On the 3rd December gunmen approached the Hope Road complex and fired a series of bullets into the house, injuring Marley, Rita and the Wailers manager Don Taylor.

Two days later Marley appeared at the concert. The shooting had of course been headline news and there was widespread speculation that he would not show up for the gig or that if he did he would perform just one song. Instead after defiantly opening his shirt to show the crowd his injuries, he ran through a set that lasted for 90 minutes. He would later launch a no holds barred attack on the paymasters responsible for the shooting in the lyrics of Ambush in the Night a track that appeared on the Survival album.

8. Exodus

WITHIN DAYS OF the concert Marley had fled on a plane to London accompanied by The Wailers' artistic director Neville Garrick. Shortly afterwards, the entire band relocated to the UK where Marley rented a dwelling in Chelsea and the Wailers did what they could to re-create the Hope Road vibe. Eager to retain their physical fitness the routine included regular football matches in Battersea Park. Garrick even claims that they played against and 'whupped some National Front guys a couple of times'.

Marley continued to work prodigiously, writing and recording Exodus which was released in June 1977. It opens with Natural Mystic a song that at first seems to invoke the myths and spirits of Jamaican legend, but concludes with Marley proposing that 'One and all got to face reality now.' Meanwhile Guiltiness rails against the rich:

Who live lives of false pretence every day
These are the big fish
Who always try to eat down the small fish.
They would do anything
To materialise their every wish.

In The Heathen he advises his brethren in no uncertain terms about what they should do to their oppressors, 'back dey pun de wall'. This was as emphatic a declaration as his call to 'chase those crazy baldheads out of town' that he had made on the stand out track from the previous year's Rastaman

Vibration. The title track on Exodus meanwhile is celebratory, triumphantly imagining the great day involving the 'movement of Jah people'. This theme is continued at the start of Side Two with the thumping, rhythm of Jamming. It is a classic tune ever popular at clubs which encourages followers to dance, an important aspect of many African rituals.

No Woman, No Cry: Rita, Cindy & Bob too

The next two tracks on Exodus are Waiting in Vain and Turn Your Lights Down Low. Along with No Woman No Cry from the previous album and Stir it Up they are arguably the most beautiful love songs Marley ever wrote. Apparently they were not written for Rita however but for the Canadian-Jamaican model Cindy Breakspeare. She had been voted Miss World at the 1976 beauty pageant in London and was in the midst of her year basking in the glory of this success. This coincided with Marley's own growing reputation and when the news of their love affair broke it sparked lurid tabloid headlines including 'Beauty and the Beast' and 'Miss World's Wild Man'. The high profile nature of Bob and Cindy's relationship, must have been astonishingly painful for Rita. By this stage however she was used to Marley's affairs and considered herself to be as his much 'guardian angel' as his wife.[42]

Both women's loyalty to Marley was astonishing and absolute. Rita and Bob met as teenagers in Trenchtown but it was not love at first sight. She admits that she was one of those people who were initially suspicious off him on account of his light skin. Her concern was that this would give him an air of unwarranted superiority. Once they got together however she developed a commitment which barely wavered throughout their time together and continued after his death. They married on the 11th February 1966, but it was soon after this that he moved to find work and live with his mother in the United States.

Following Bob's return Rita worked hard to support the family while he struggled to make it. She was a promising performer herself but like so many women, she sacrificed her own career in order to look after their children. Eventually she put her efforts to forge a solo career of her own to one side and instead joined his band as a backing singer.

After originally relocating to Nassau in the aftermath of the Hope Road shooting Rita returned to Jamaica partly for the sake of their children's education while Bob departed for England. Moreover she knew that he was spending much of his time with Breakspeare and that her love rival was angling for him to marry her. Indeed she expected it to happen whilst Cindy, who would soon become pregnant with Marley's child was blissfully unaware that he was even married.

In her account of their life together Rita suggests that Bob justified his infidelity in the following terms:

> Baby, you couldn't have all the babies that I feel I should have. I don't want to get you pregnant every year. So some of that is really just taking the burden off you and your body.[43]

She admitted in the book that her husband's behaviour frustrated her and that she 'felt unfulfilled and sometimes used.'[44] Not only did Bob have numerous affairs and other baby mothers, he also sought to block her later efforts to carve out an independent career for herself. Nevertheless she handled all of this with considerable dignity. She stuck with him, even agreeing to take in some of the children he fathered with other women in order to ensure that they had a more comfortable upbringing.

During Bob's final illness Rita shared nursing and family

duties with Cindy who remained a constant and loving presence in Marley's life even though he never did divorce Rita and marry her as she had hoped. Together the two women undertook the poignant task of cutting off Bob's locks as his body became increasingly weak. In the final hours though it was Rita who was by his bedside and who tied a red, black and green ribbon around his head after he had drawn his final breath.

Given all the sacrifices that she made for Bob, Rita must have been heartbroken when she first heard Turn Your Lights Down Low and Waiting in Vain and it has been suggested that she always refused to perform them.

The second album which was largely conceived and written whilst Marley was in Britain was Kaya released in 1978. It is one of his least celebrated works, which many reviewers have derided for being soft. Blackwell cites it as his favourite however and argues that it was not simply a ganga fuelled chill out disc. Instead it was conceived as a record invoking love and harmony with the aim of soothing the strife that was devastating so many lives back at home. The opening track Easy Skanking is surely a nod to Beckford's groundbreaking Easy Snappin' and the album progresses in a relatively laid back groove. It concludes though with two songs which clearly demonstrate where Marley's head and heart lay, Running Away and the mesmeric Time Will Tell.

Return: One love peace concert

Time had not brought an end to the gang warfare back in Jamaica though. Arguably it had got even worse in the intervening period. Macdonald's documentary includes some shocking images of the running street battles that were leading to so much death and destruction. It was in these seemingly hopeless circumstances that members of the rival gangs turned to Marley for help.

By now, with a number of critically acclaimed albums under his belt Marley was clearly the real deal; a bona fide superstar. But he was also still a modest and generous man who remembered his roots and had remained friends with people on both sides of the divide. The gangs were increasingly desperate to bring the spiral of violence to an end and began to canvass the idea of some sort of truce. Bucky Marshall who was affiliated to the PNP and Claudie Massop a supporter of the JLP had encountered each other in prison and it was there that they came up with the idea of asking Marley to headline a concert that was aimed at bringing peace and reconciliation. He agreed, returned to a triumphant welcome in February 1978 and the final plans were made for the April 22nd gathering.

Marley's appearance at what became known as the One Love Peace Concert resulted in one of the most iconic images in Jamaican history. He had been preceded by his former bandmate Tosh, who had by now adopted the Ethiopian name Wolde Semayat. Timothy White suggests that when he ascended the stage the one time Wailer defiantly lit up a spliff, took advantage of the opportunity to denounce the hypocrisy of Manley and Seaga and attacked the 'shitstem' over which they presided.[45]

Marley's approach was very different. Midway through his performance of Jamming, he paused and called the rival leaders up onto the stage. Still smarting from Tosh's attack they shuffled hesitantly towards each other on either side of Marley. Suddenly Marley seized the right hands of the two men who towered over him and held them together and aloft in a gesture of unity. It was a remarkable intervention from one who was so sceptical about politicians. It was not for Manley and Seaga of course but rather for the people of the island who he so cherished. It is a measure of his status that nobody else could have done what he did on that thunderous night.

Sadly Marley's symbolic act did not bring an end to the conflict. Nine months later Massop died in a shoot out with the police near Marcus Garvey Drive in the Denham Town area. Marshall was also to die in a hail of bullets though not in Jamaica but, rather at a reggae 'jump up' in Brooklyn, New York in May 1980. Meanwhile 900 people died as a result of acts of political violence in the run up to the 1980 elections which delivered a landslide victory for Seaga.

9. African independence

MARLEY'S 1980 ALBUM Survival proudly displays the flags of 48 African countries alongside the image of a slaveship which highlighted the sacrifices made by the people of the continent. It marked a return to the militancy displayed on the first side of Exodus and showed that despite the demoralising aftermath of the One Love Concert, Marley's commitment to the struggle remained undimmed. He was undoubtedly a global star now but his mission was far from complete. Survival was arguably his most direct, explicit and important call for independence to date. He welcomed the band's popularity in Europe and America but his real mission was to unite to 'all Africans'. Indeed, Africa Unite was the self-explanatory title of the track which opened Side Two.

The album begins though by setting the scene with a declaration that there is 'So much trouble in the world'. It continues with a series of songs that rail against the Babylon system. The track of that name includes some of Marley's most profound insights, words which call to mind the famous declaration by Malcolm X that capitalism is a system of bloodsuckers:

> Babylon system is the vampire
> Sucking the blood of the sufferers
> Building church and university
> Deceiving the people continually
> Me say dem graduating thieves and murderers
> Look out now
> Sucking the blood of the sufferers

Zimbabwe

Unperturbed by his earlier calamitous association with politically charged events, it was Survival that gave rise to what would turn out to be Marley's final overtly political appearance. One of the tracks on the album was entitled Zimbabwe and was dedicated to the struggle to overthrow minority rule in the southern African country Rhodesia. The song was enthusiastically adopted by the liberation movement and consequently, The Wailers were invited by the newly elected Prime Minister Robert Mugabe to perform at the inaugural ceremony where the old colonial flag was lowered and Rhodesia became Zimbabwe, the latest African country to gain independence. Marley was so thrilled by this invitation that he forked out the shipping costs of the band's equipment himself when his prospective hosts baulked at the price putting the proposal in jeopardy.

Once again as with Smile Jamaica in 1976, things did not go as well as might have been hoped. Denise Mills a leading executive at Island Records recalls that the travelling party were met off the aeroplane by the new Home Affairs Minister

Joshua Nkomo and ferried to a palace where they were regaled by drunken soldiers and fed cucumber sandwiches and lemonade, 'so English and colonial' she remarks, 'all considered a bit off by the Wailers'.[46]

Following their arrival at the venue where the ceremony was to take place matters descended even further. The Wailers discovered that whilst the outgoing Governor-General, His Excellency The Lord Soames and Prince Charles were welcome guests, the masses who had fought the fight against imperial oppression were made to huddle outside the stadium. Not surprisingly once the pomp of the official

handover had finished and the band began to strike up, the people decided to take matters into their own hands, stormed through the locked gates and began running joyously towards the stage.

What happened next was an ominous foretaste of what was to come not just in Mugabe's Zimbabwe but across the continent. The incoming crowd was sent fleeing in fear as the police wielded batons and fired tear gas in an effort to drive them back to their allotted place. Footage of the concert shows members of the band including Marley himself reeling from the effects of the fumes but like a true champion he decided that the show must go on.

As the Wailers returned to the stage Marley turned to his band and declared 'Now I know who the real revolutionaries are'. Once again, it was for the people not the dignitaries that he was performing and, indeed, following that debacle, the band agreed to put on a show the following night and did so to an estimated crowd of 100,000.

Bob Marley: Roots, Reggae & Revolution

Thirty-five years on, Robert Mugabe by now in his 90s remained in office. Not content with the lowly title of prime minister, he had created and elevated himself to the position of president. His decades in power were marked by obscene levels of personal enrichment, the favouring of a tiny elite, continued misery for the masses and brutal repression meted out to anyone who dared to oppose this state of affairs.

Many of the street names in downtown Harare, the capital of Zimbabwe are named after the freedom fighters who led heroic struggles against colonialism, men such as Kwame Nkrumah, Julius Nyerere, Nelson Mandela, Samora Machel and Kenneth Kaunda the liberation leaders of Ghana, Tanzania, South Africa, Mozambique and Zambia respectively. As with Mugabe however once they had moved from opposition to elected office these activists failed to deliver true equality and prosperity for their people.

A stroll down those very same Harare streets exposes the chasm between the rich and poor. By day the privileged elite, many of them black, dressed in their finery do business in plush air conditioned offices. As dusk settles, they are replaced by a mass of poor people drifting in to hawk and hustle whatever they can lay their hands on. With their international banks and hotels, the streets look like those of any modern capital yet when I visited the city 30 years after independence there were power cuts every single day. Invariably they would occur towards the end of the working day and lasted through the night. It is a desperate situation which is expected to continue well into the next decade. The rich have generators at home and are therefore too lazy and complacent to address the issue. The poor meanwhile are exiled to the city's outskirts and have to cook and eat early and survive by candlelight.

Had he lived, Marley would surely have railed against the

likes of Mugabe, Africa's so called 'Big Men' who have looted their own economies and totally betrayed the masses. Mandela was an honourable exception, but even his presidency was a disappointment and his successors Thabo Mbeki and Jacob Zuma have taken their lead from their neighbouring kleptocrats. Ever thoughtful and challenging, Marley would have sides with the 'downpressed' and wondered why the Big Men act this way, 'Ah wah mek dem a gwan so?'.

Those words feature in One Drop, just one of the brilliant tracks that appears on Survival. It is a another carefully constructed song whose title refers to the distinctive drumming style pioneered by Carlton Barrett. It is not just a throwaway title though. The words focus on the spiritual importance of drumming and Marley encourages us to 'feel it in the one drop' and through this he asserts we will find our redemption:

So feel this drumbeat
I tell you what, it's beating within
Feel your heart playing a rhythm
And you know it's resisting against ism and skism[47]

There is of course another meaning to the term 'one drop' which will not be lost on students of race. The notion that anyone with one drop of black blood should be classified – and discriminated against – was established in the 1800s and codified in the United States as late as the 20th century.

The subject matter of Survival is an indication of how Marley was increasingly exploring themes that were wider than the island of his birth. A later example is the popular posthumous hit Buffalo Soldier which considered the plight of the black American regiments that were established in the aftermath of the Civil War. It highlights again the fact that Marley was a more profound thinker than many give him credit for.

10. Redemption Song – a last testament

THE BAND'S FOLLOW up to Survival was Uprising another album which contains some wonderful music. One song stands out above all others however. Once again it is a track in which the artist searches for atonement and solace and this time it is boldly stated in the simple two world title: Redemption Song. The version that appeared on the original vinyl release sounds unlike almost anything released in Marley's name either before or since. It is a simple but beautiful song; one on which the artist lays himself bare. It certainly can't be described as reggae. The instrumentation is stripped right back as the bandleader alone strums an acoustic guitar. He mixes Garvey's words from a 1937 speech with his own lyrics, urging his brethren to 'Emancipate yourselves from mental slavery. None but ourselves can free our minds'

The album was released in the summer of 1980 and as was customary, the band embarked on a major tour to promote it. Sadly Marley was never able to complete the schedule. He collapsed while out running in Central Park, New York during the United States leg and a hospital appointment confirmed the terrible news that his body was now ravaged with cancer. An initial diagnosis had been made back in 1977 when Marley injured a toe playing football.

There are conflicting claims that he was told that the toe or alternatively, his entire leg needed to be amputated. Similarly, there is disagreement as to whether he resisted for religious reasons or because it would prevent him playing his beloved sport. Either way nothing was done and tragically, by the spring of 1981 Bob's fate was sealed. He died in a Miami clinic on the 11th May at the tender age of 36. *Uprising* was therefore to be the band's final studio release during Bob's lifetime and Redemption Song stands as a poignant last testament.

Marley and the black British diaspora

The Wailers' international breakthrough was hugely important not just for Marley, his fellow band members or for Jamaica generally. It had a resonance throughout the Caribbean Diaspora not least in Britain and not only for those who had upped sticks and relocated to the UK but also for those of us who were born on these islands.

Masters of the Soul also includes footage of the Windrush pioneers disembarking in Tilbury, East London. The most memorable moment comes when the interviewer speaks to a smart suited young man named Alwyn Roberts. As it happens, Roberts was one of the few travellers who was not from Jamaica. He was from Trinidad and was better known as the Calypso singer 'Lord Kitchener'. When invited 'Kitch' could not resist the opportunity to display his prowess and burst into a rendition of 'London is the place for me'

The full version of his song about 'this lovely city' continues:

> *To live in London you are really comfortable*
> *Because the English people are very much sociable*
> *They take you here and they take you there*
> *And they make you feel like a millionaire*[48]

The reality for those that arrived both on the *Empire Windrush* and in the years that followed is that, far from receiving a warm welcome in the 'Mother Country' they were met with hostility, discrimination and violence. When they went in search of somewhere to live they were confronted by signs declaring 'No blacks, no dogs, no Irish.' Employment was plentiful but in the dirtiest, least prestigious and lowest paid jobs and they were shunned by trade unions which bought into the divisive agenda that they and their Irish brethren posed a threat to the livelihood of British born workers. In short, they were trapped in a vicious circle of institutional racism long before it was officially acknowledged by the 1999 Stephen Lawrence Inquiry Report.

Notting Hill was one of the areas where the racial violence was worst. A series of riots broke out in August and September 1958 encouraged by the likes of Oswald Mosley's British Union of Fascists and the White Defence League. Less than a year later, on the 17th May 1959, Kelso Cochrane, an Antiguan carpenter was stabbed to death by a racist gang. Emboldened by this racism, Mosley stood in the 1959 general election for the Kensington North seat which included the area winning 8.1 percent.

Those pioneers did not simply take their licks lying down however. It takes a great deal of resourcefulness to up sticks and relocate to a different country. They also have brought with them a knowledge of the struggles that were taking place in their own islands; struggles which in many cases would soon lead to independence.

Rather than capitulating in the face of violence and discrimination, they stood up, fought back and demanded respect and recognition. Madge Dresser's excellent pamphlet *Black and White on the Buses* tells the story of one of the first black led campaign against racial discrimination in this period.[49] It demonstrates how black workers in Bristol had to struggle not just against their employers, but the unions, churches and city council. That they succeeded and, in so doing, demanded and won the respect of their local MP Tony Benn, white workers and the ultimately the Transport and General Workers Union is a measure of their determination.

The same is true of the origins of the Notting Hill Carnival. Today it is lauded as Europe's biggest street party and no news report is complete without footage of the police mixing easily with the revellers. As we have seen this was not always the case and still today the positive reports are mixed with bulletins detailing how the police have cracked down on criminal gangs supposedly intent on spoiling everybody else's fun. The truth is that Carnival itself is the product of struggle. It did not simply come about by chance.

Central to founding the Carnival was Claudia Jones who had been born in Trinidad in 1915 and become active in the Communist Party in Harlem after her family moved to the United States. This led to her deportation to Britain in 1955 from where she went on to establish the *West Indian Gazette* with the aim of 'serving as a catalyst, quickening awareness, socially and politically, of West Indians and Afro-Asians in Britain, for peace and friendship between all Commonwealth and world peoples.'

Jones suffered from poor health throughout her life, but it was typical of her that she fought tirelessly against discrimination, including the 1962 Immigration Act, and for reconciliation. Black activists and anti-racists had fought for unity in the aftermath of Kelso Cochrane's death and, as a result, his funeral was marked by a crowd of over 1,200 and his grave bears the inscription 'From the Trades Council and his West Indian friends'.

It is typical of Claudia Jones that her response to the race riots of 1958 was to propose a Carnival that would bring the tradition of her country to the UK. The first such event was a modest gathering in St Pancras Hall in 1959. Subsequently it became a grander affair with sound systems, floats and other paraphernalia. celebrating music and culture from across the islands.[50]

Many if not most of those who moved to Britain never intended to remain permanently. Instead, their aim was to stay for a few years, make good money and also learn new skills and ideas which they could take back and place at the service of their own newly independent countries. Much of what they earned would be sent home to support their families and, as it turned out, the struggling economies of those islands. Some of it though was intended to buy a plot of land upon which to build a home for when they themselves returned after a few years.

As the decades rolled by it became clear that this dream would remain beyond the reach of increasing numbers. As their hopes of an early return faded therefore the black presence in Britain became more established and permanent and inevitably therefore relationships formed and couples began to have families.

Notting Hill Carnival on a grand scale, but also the smaller community events and house parties that were organised enabled people to come together and feel better about their predicament as they listened and danced to the music of the

Caribbean.

Notting Hill continued to be a site of major battles. For two decades from the early 1970s, the police waged a campaign against Frank Critchlow the proprietor of the Mangrove restaurant on All Saints Road. Critchlow was no ordinary restaurateur however and Mangrove was no ordinary restaurant. Rather he was a community activist committed to fighting injustice both internationally, South African apartheid in particular, and in Britain and his premises became something of an organising centre for community campaigns. Consequently he came in for hostile attention from the police who raided it twelve times between January 1969 and July 1970, claiming that it was a 'haunt for criminals, prostitutes and ponces'. The community responded to this harassment with a small demonstration at the end of which 19 people were arrested and charged with a variety of offences including conspiracy to riot, affray and assaulting police officers.

The campaign to defend those charged, the Mangrove Nine, which included Critchlow, Darcus Howe and Barbara Beese proved to be a landmark case in British legal history. Working alongside a team of radical lawyers, they fought hard for a fair trial demanding a jury of their peers. After 55 days, justice prevailed and the defendants walked free from the Old Bailey, the most senior criminal court in the country.

The harassment continued right through until 1989 however. In that year Michael Mansfield QC successfully defended Critchlow against a charge of supplying heroin. The Deputy Assistant Commissioner responsible for West London by this time was Paul Condon who went on to become the Metropolitan Police Commissioner shortly before Stephen Lawrence's death. It was he who, at the time of the Stephen Lawrence Inquiry, steadfastly refused to acknowledge the existence of institutional racism within his organisation's ranks.

The recognition by Sir William Macpherson that it did in fact pervade the police force was the culmination of decades of determined struggle by black communities and their allies. These were struggles that had taken in the case of the Mangrove Nine, the New Cross Fire of 1981, and the riots that had erupted in places such as Brixton, Toxteth in Liverpool and Tottenham in 1981 and 1985. These struggles were an indication of the fact that institutional racism was blighting the lives of a new generation of black people; a generation who had been born on these shores.

As we have noted, the dashed hopes of a prosperous return had led to the establishment of more permanent black communities and in turn therefore, the formation of families. By the late 1960s, the first generation of children born to that immigrant generation were completing their compulsory education with alarming results. Their parents had high expectations of them but instead of fulfilling them, huge numbers of black children were emerging with substandard grades. It was in these circumstances that a group of parents and activists commissioned a groundbreaking study by Grenadian scholar Bernard Coard which was published as a pamphlet in 1971 under the title *How The West Indian Child is Made Educationally Subnormal in the British School System.*[51]

To this day and despite the efforts of many community activists and both black and white teachers and unions the discrimination that Coard's pamphlet exposed has never been fully addressed. Its consequences can be witnessed in the continued marginalisation and exclusion of black communities. In the 1970s this was compounded by the fact that there were very few people that looked like them who young black people could aspire to emulate.

Too much can be made of so called 'role models' but it is

undoubtedly the case that young people's aspirations are shaped, at least in part, by the achievements of those who have gone before them. Invariably when young people are told to look up to their "elders and betters" though it is to 'professionals', bankers, lawyers and military personnel or authority figures who reinforce a traditional and conservative view of society.

There is no way that the Establishment would have chosen a militant, marijuana smoking Rastafarian as a role model for black British youth but that is what Bob Marley became. He had made it; nobody could deny that he was a success and we wanted to bask in that glory. But he had also done it by being tough and unapologetic, by expressing and articulating the pain of the 'sufferers' and by challenging the very oppression that blighted us all. It is little wonder that a generation of young people whose parents weren't even from Jamaica and who had never been to the island started locksing up and speaking patois.

It is no exaggeration to say that reggae provided the soundtrack to the uprisings in the 1970s and 80s that we have highlighted. It was the music that best expressed the anger and alienation experienced by that generation. The words of Burnin' and Lootin' the fourth track on Burnin are ones with which many of the rebellious youth could readily identify":

This morning I woke up in a curfew
Oh God I was a prisoner too
Could not recognise the faces standing over me
All dressed in uniforms of brutality
How many rivers do we have to cross
Before we can talk to the boss?
All that we got, it seems we have lost
We must have really paid the cost
That's why we're gonna be

Bob Marley: Roots, Reggae & Revolution

Burnin' and lootin' tonight
Burnin' and lootin' tonight
Burnin' all pollution tonight
Burnin' all illusion tonight.

However, for some West Indians of an older generation who had grown up on calypso, the appeal of reggae and Marley's music was harder to fathom. As we have discovered, C.L.R. James was not one to downplay the achievements of his Caribbean brethren. When invited to comment on Marley's passing, James – now living in Brixton – acknowledged the artist's significance, but was was less than effusive in his praise:

> For the first time a West Indian had made an international contribution which was not based on an intellectual understanding. For the first time this had come from below, and I want to make it clear that nobody could understand the Rastas unless they understood mass life. That was an astonishing business not only for the world but for West Indians themselves. The Rastas were saying things that, although sometimes absurd, had value in that they were opposed to the European attitudes, European power that had dominated West Indian life for so long. That the music could become an international movement was not in the mind of the Caribbean people. Not only did it come from them, but it was accepted by the mass of the population in Britain. There of all places! They are a not a people who have a tradition of jazz.[52]

11. Rock Against Racism

It is worth recalling in some detail the circumstances in which one of the great cultural movements in 20th century Britain, Rock against Racism (RAR) came into being. On the 5th August 1976 rock guitarist Eric Clapton, once regarded himself as a living god by admirers of his musical virtuosity, launched into an alcohol-fuelled tirade during a performance at the Birmingham Odeon. At the end of an outburst which included several references to 'coons' and 'black wogs' he declared that 'Enoch was right'.

The person he was referring to, Enoch Powell had been a leading figure in the British Conservative Party and a minister in the 1960-63 government. Moreover, as Health Minister in 1963, his solution to a shortage of doctors in the new and expanding National Health Service was to invite medics from the Caribbean to come over and apply their skills in the UK. It was not this encouragement of immigration however that Clapton was referring to.

By 1968, Powell was singing a very different tune. He was by now a diminished figure thwarted in his efforts to win the Tory leadership and in a desperate bid to restore his popularity he decided to make a carefully orchestrated pitch to the racist right. On the 20th April 1968 this much admired 'classical scholar' delivered a widely trailed speech on immigration in which he declared that 'As I look ahead, I am filled with foreboding; like the Roman, I seem to see the River Tiber foaming with much blood.'

Beneath the fancy language lay a series of lies and exaggerated claims which were so inflammatory that the Tory leader Edward Heath felt compelled to sack him from the Shadow

Cabinet. Powell never held a senior political position again but instead of disappearing into obscurity these words catapulted him into the unofficial position of Britain's Racist-in-Chief. Within days of his foul outburst, groups of workers including dockers in East London and meat porters at Smithfield Market in Central London had marched in support of him.

In the years that followed anyone wishing to parade their racist credentials would refer to Powell. Britain's black communities hated him. The mere mention of his name provoked anger and resentment amongst people who had been encouraged to come over and re-build the 'Mother Country' in the aftermath of the Second World War. No less a person than the supposedly sweet, innocent little Millie Small stopped focusing on how her heart had been made 'giddy up' by her boy lollipop. Instead, her 1970 album Time Will Tell included a track entitled Enoch Power.

Clapton has never offered an unequivocal apology for his outburst. Many years later the most that he would admit was that he had been drunk but he continued to lament a 'loss of tradition' and 'English identity'. As recently as 2004 in an *Uncut* magazine interview and again on the British TV programme The *South Bank Show* in 2007, he was defending Powell, describing him as 'outrageously brave'.[53] At best the guitarist has hidden behind the fact that his music is predominantly derived from the Blues, the classic black American genre, to demonstrate his progressive credentials.

It should be noted that Clapton was not the only pop star whose antics in this period were, at best, grossly irresponsible. That very same year David Bowie allegedly gave a Nazi salute to fans who had arrived to greet him at Victoria Station. There followed a foul interview with *Playboy* magazine during which he suggested that 'Adolf Hitler was one of the first rock stars'. Nor were these isolated observations. Two years earlier he had declared 'Britain is ready for a Fascist leader...I think that Britain could really benefit from a fascist leader'. To be fair to Bowie, he did subsequently express remorse, attributing his behaviour to a debilitating addiction to drugs and he would go on to marry the Somalian model Iman Abdulmajid.

The mid 1970s was no time for such loose talk or provocative gestures. This was a period of economic stagnation and deep social divisions in Britain. A massive upsurge in industrial action had brought down Heath's government in 1974. It was replaced by a Labour administration which failed to fulfil the aspirations of its working class supporters. As the economy ground to a halt in that pivotal year 1976, the Chancellor of the Exchequer Denis Healey went cap in hand to the International Monetary Fund for a bailout loan. The price for this was to be deep cuts in public expenditure which once again inflamed working people and led to strife, division and bitter struggles.

In these grim circumstances, racism was on the rise as opportunists, populists and outright fascists sought to scapegoat foreigners for the economic malaise. The National Front was one such group and like others, they took their lead from Powell. Just months before Clapton's tirade, Powell was at it again, telling an audience which was bigger than that for his 'Rivers of Blood' speech that Britain was 'still being eroded and hollowed out from within by alien wedges'. It is in this context therefore that we must consider Clapton's tirade and Bowie's flirtations.

The 'rock god' had enjoyed considerable success in the 1960s in bands such as The Yardbirds, John Mayall's Bluesbreakers albeit briefly, and the 'supergroup' Cream. He had even recorded with The Beatles, playing lead guitar on the George

Harrison composition While My Guitar Gently Weeps. By the mid-70s however Clapton's brand of rock/blues had been marginalised and he was in the doldrums. The song that did most to revive his flagging career was none other than a cover version of Marley's I Shot the Sheriff. As with his earlier success therefore, it was his take on ostensibly 'black' music which restored his fortunes.

Not surprisingly, the outburst captured headlines and consequently, the attention of a wider audience then those who had witnessed it first-hand. They included two young music fans Roger Huddle, a member of the International Socialists, the forerunner to today's Socialist Workers Party and Red Saunders, IS supporter, photographer and agit-prop theatre performer. They responded by writing a letter to the *New Musical Express* magazine which stated:

> Come on Eric…you've been taking too much of that *Daily Express* stuff and you know you can't handle it. Own up. Half of your music is black. You're rock music's biggest colonist. You're a good musician but where would you be without the Blues and R&B? You've got to fight the racist poison otherwise you degenerate into the sewer with the rats and all the money men who ripped off rock culture with their cheque books and plastic crap. We want to organise a rank-and-file movement against the racist poisoning music. We urge support for Rock against Racism. PS: Who shot the Sheriff Eric? It sure as hell wasn't you![54]

From this little spark a huge flame was ignited. The response to the letter was so overwhelming that its authors decided to set RAR up as a movement. In the years that followed it would play a critical role in transforming the lives of a generation of young people.

The establishment of RAR prefigured some key developments

that were occurring in the British music scene. At one extreme, the glam rock which had dominated the pop charts in the early 70s was being challenged by a grittier form of music in the shape of punk rock. Elsewhere white youth were listening to the reggae of artists such as Marley and mixing with their black counterparts in clubs where soul, R&B and ska were hugely popular. It could only be a matter of time before such influences began to reflect themselves in the music that these young people made as they formed bands of their own.

Punk rock was the archetypal anti-establishment music. It was anarchic, vulgar and often deliberately tuneless. The Sex Pistols chart topping, Silver Jubilee busting 1977 single God Save the Queen and the images of Britain's monarch with a safety pin through her nose were the most vivid expression of this. Many of us who witnessed it will never forget the band's notorious expletive laden appearance on the early evening Thames Television programme *Today* in December 1976. These angry white proponents of punk found themselves in common cause with their black brethren who were fighting back against the 'uniforms of brutality' who were systematically using medieval stop and search laws to harass, bully and oppress them.

Black British artists, inspired by the example of Marley and his compatriot and sometime mentor Jimmy Cliff began to articulate these examples of institutional racism. Prominent among them were Aswad, Misty in Roots, Steel Pulse and dub poet Linton Kwesi Johnson himself. In turn, groups of young white musicians started to sympathise and draw parallels with their own experiences. Hence, The Clash a band formed in the very same West London streets where Carnival took place called for a White Riot to match those that black youth were involved in and recorded their own version of reggae star Junior Murvin's Police and Thieves.[55]

Young London reggae band Aswad *play Rock Against Racism's May Day gig at the Roundhouse 1977. Also playing were funk band* Limousine *and theatre group* Kartoon Klowns. *All women Punk band* The Slits *joined jam session at end of night along with Paul Jones from* Manfred Mann *on harmonica.*

Elsewhere the fusion was even more pronounced. Much of the best and most popular music of the late 1970s and early 80s was made by bands whose members were drawn from both communities and who played their own updated version of the ska they had heard in clubs or on their parents turntables. Pre-eminent among them was The Specials, a band set up in Coventry by keyboard player Jerry Dammers. It was he who coined the term 'Two Tone' and set up a label which housed a number of other multiracial groups including The Beat and The Selector.

The founders of RAR realised that the fruits of this culture clash did not automatically flow one way however. A number of the very same bands that performed under the Two Tone banner, notably Madness and Bad Manners had a significant following among organised fascist groups. Meanwhile the NF tried to claim that punk was authentic 'white folk music' and Paul Gilroy notes that both The Clash and The Stranglers who recorded a song entitled I Feel Like a Wog regularly featured in the NF's *Bulldog* newspaper Rock Against Communism chart.[56] Elsewhere Meanwhile Dammers recalls that The Specials first tour as a support band in 1978 was disrupted by fascist skinheads associated with headline act Sham 69.

Recognising that this was contested territory, RAR sought to draw white youth away from the racists by highlighting the black origins of much of the music that they were revelling in. Over a 4 year period, it organised over 200 events across Britain and every single one aimed to showcase a diverse range of artists united around the rallying slogan 'Love Music, Hate Racism'. The same was true of its counter cultural magazine *Temporary Hoarding* which sought to carry the same message in both written and visual form.

RAR is best known for two huge Carnivals it organised in conjunction with the newly formed Anti Nazi League (ANL) in April and September 1978 in Victoria Park and Brockwell Park in East and South London respectively. The line-ups for these mass gatherings brilliantly illustrates the movement's unifying aim. The headline acts in Victoria Park were X Ray Spex, The Clash, The Tom Robinson Band and Steel Pulse. The line-up for the September event included Aswad, Sham 69, Misty in Roots and Elvis Costello and the Attractions.

Some of the finest music of the era directly addressed the question of defeating the Nazis. One of Steel Pulse's most famous songs was Jah Pickney RAR. Its lyrics made it clear what Jah's children (pickney) should do:

> *I've come to conclusion that*
> *We're gonna hunt the National Front*
> *We're gonna hunt the National Front*
> *Cos they believe in apartheid*
> *For that we're gonna whop their hides*
> *For all my people they cheated and lied*
> *I won't rest til I'm satisfied*[57]

Linton Linton Kwesi Johnson was not just a commentator but, rather a major cultural figure much of whose poetry was performed to music produced by Dennis Bovell. Reggae Fi Peach is dedicated to Blair Peach, a mixed race teacher who was bludgeoned to death by the police on an anti NF demonstration in Southall on the 23rd April 1979. Meanwhile Misty in Roots, were a Southall based collective whose studio provided a community centre for local youth. On that very same day their studio was raided by the police, equipment smashed and the band's manager Clarence Baker spent four weeks in hospital after being beaten about the head. He subsequently found himself alongside six members of the band and a number of others in the dock, charged with violence and obstruction.

Alongside the ANL and other anti-racists, RAR undoubtedly

had a profound effect in helping to turn the tide against the NF. In the period leading up to and including the year of the Carnivals, the fascists were clearly on the rise. Indeed NF leader Martin Webster later argued that that they were on the verge of power. Though this was a wildly exaggerated claim it was certainly true that they were regularly beating the then Liberal Party in the polls. In 1976 they grabbed nearly 20 percent of the vote in local elections in Leicester and the following year gained over 119,000 votes in the Greater London Council elections.

By 1981 however the NF was in serious decline. It soon fell apart and its successor the British National Party has never been able to emulate the achievements of the 1970s. This was not simply a random occurrence. Instead what stopped them in their tracks was a united front built from the bottom up which brought black and white people together. The organised working class, including many from the same workplaces that had marched in support of Powell in 1968, were key alongside many thousands of young people who cut their political teeth through their involvement in Rock Against Racism.

Arguably the most prominent name missing from the line up at either carnival was Bob Marley. This is not because he was unaware or indifferent to the cultural developments that were occurring. One song that does not appear on any original album but was released as a 12 inch (extended) single and was later included on CD reissues of Exodus is Punky Reggae Party recorded in 1977. Its lyrics refer to an imaginary gathering of bands including The Damned, The Clash and Dr Feelgood. Alongside them are Toots and the Maytals one of the finest bands from the Trojan Records label whose music appeared on the soundtrack to arguably the most famous ever Jamaican film *The Harder They Come*.[58] Marley also assures us that 'The Wailers will be there' before declaring hilariously that 'no boring old farts will be there'. One hopes that this was a sideswipe at the likes of Eric Clapton.

The fact that Marley never played a RAR gig is one of the great lost opportunities. In 1982 Red Saunders travelled to Jamaica in order to shoot a photo story for the *Sunday Times*. During the trip he was shown around the Tuff Gong studio by the I-Threes and noticed that there, on the wall of Bob's office was a mounted copy of the letter that had launched RAR. We will never know of course, but given Bob's nature and the generosity with which he gave of himself we can but speculate that he would have jumped at the chance to perform in front of an appreciative RAR crowd. Wonderful though their achievements were, Saunders and Huddle rued the fact that they never asked Marley and John Lennon to headline one of their great festivals.

Babylon

The National Front certainly did have their hides whopped but of course this did not bring an end to the wider marginalisation of black youth. Inevitably therefore most of the output of these black British groups focused on wider experiences of life in 'Babylon'. That was in fact the title of a 1980 film starring Aswad's lead singer Brinsley Forde. Driven on by a Dennis Bovell soundtrack and featuring Aswad's classic Warrior Charge it explores sound system culture and the struggle to escape poverty as its protagonists hustle around south London's mean streets trying to avoid the police and strive to make it in the music business.

Another of Aswad's finest songs African Children focused on the pain of displacement:

African children
In a concrete situation
African children
Wonder do they know where you're coming from
All of the nation are living in these tenements
Precast stonewall concrete cubicles
Their rent increases each and every other day
Structural repairs are assessed yet not done
Lift out of action on the twenty-seventh floor
And when they work they smell
African children
Living in a concrete situation[59]

On a similar theme, Steel Pulse released songs such as Prodigal Son and Babylon Makes the Rules which encouraged their brethren to 'recapture our culture' whilst the albums True Democracy and Tribute to the Martyrs paid homage to freedom fighters such as George Jackson, Garvey and Steve Biko. Sonny's Lettah by Linton Kwesi Johnson captures the harsh reality of life for black youth at the hands of the criminal justice system and Inglan is a Bitch is a damning indictment of late 20th century Britain; a far cry from London is the Place for Me.

Such alienation was not simply the case for black youth however. The early 80s uprisings are habitually referred to as race riots, but this was not in fact the case. The concrete misery explored by Aswad and visualised in Babylon was the common experience of working class black and white youth in Margaret Thatcher's Britain. Its bleakness was brilliantly captured by The Specials in Ghost Town a haunting tune which focused on the devastation of their home city:

This town, is coming like a ghost town
All the clubs are being closed down
This place, is coming like a ghost town

> *Bands won't play no more*
> *Too much fighting on the dance floor*[60]

Ghost Town was unquestionably the song of the summer in 1981. Released at a time when the streets were still hot with riots, it reached Number One in July, stayed there for three weeks and remained in the charts for forty weeks in total.

As Two-Tone began to fade, Birmingham's UB40 took up the mantle. The group took its name from the unemployment benefit card that was so familiar to hundreds of thousands of disaffected youth in Margaret Thatcher's Britain. They recorded a series of politically charged albums such as their debut Signing Off and its successor Present Arms and later sought to pay homage to the canon of great Jamaican music with cover versions of classic tracks including Eric Donaldson's Cherry Oh Baby, Jimmy Cliff's wonderful Many Rivers to Cross and Marley's Keep On Moving.

12 Legacy

With Bob Marley and the Wailers very much in in the forefront then, reggae was at the cutting edge of popular music at the turn of the decade. A wealth of outstanding bands including Black Uhuru, Culture and Third World, as well as solo artists and combos such as the drum and bass duo Sly Dunbar and Robbie Shakespeare, Burning Spear (Winston Rodney) and the British bands we have previously highlighted burst onto the scene. In addition female artists, including the I-Threes themselves most notably Marcia Griffiths have stepped out, in their case literally, stepped out of the shadows and become stars in their own right.

Alongside the 'conscious' roots music, new forms emerged with the likes of Matumbi, Gregory Isaacs, Denis Brown,

Jean Adebambo and Susan Cadogan achieving success with a softer, romantic style which was known as Lovers Rock. Elsewhere, the technical wizardry of figures such as Perry and King Tubby evolved into the highly popular sub genre called 'dub'. It was this instrumental re-working of tunes which opened up space for the toasters and DJs that dominate the ragga and dancehall scene of today.

Indeed, reggae was so popular that everyone seemed to want a piece of the action. The Beatles had been early converts, but it is probably best to gloss over Ob-La-Di, Ob-La-Da and C Moon, Paul McCartney's later effort with Wings. The Rolling Stones were also fans, hanging out with Marley and recording Hey Negrita in 1976. A couple of years later lead singer Mick Jagger went on to record Walk and Don't Look Back with Peter Tosh. Elvis Costello and The Attractions released Watching the Detectives in 1977 and Blondie's version of a Paragon's ska track The Tide is High came out in 1980.

Whilst these were occasional forays by artists whose main genre was rock, a parallel development was the establishment of bands that simply appropriated the music. Hence one of the most successful all white bands of the time adopted a name that would surely alienate them from huge swathes of young black music lovers: The Police and gave their second album a pseudo-French title Regatta de Blanc which supposedly stood for 'White Reggae'.

As this brief survey of the development of reggae has shown therefore, music is constantly evolving and so it is that 30 years on, most of what we hear from the genre is very different to that which Bob Marley pioneered. By the turn of the millennium, dancehall and ragga were hugely popular but more likely to capture headlines for less savoury reasons. The lyrics of artists such as Buju Banton, Sizzla Kalonji, Vybz

Kartel and Elephant Man were relentlessly homophobic and contributed to a climate of bigotry that culminated in the murder of dozens of gay men including leading equal rights activist Brian Williamson in 2004. Since then both Kartel and Banton have been convicted in Jamaica and the USA respectively and sentenced to lengthy prison terms, Kartel for murdering an associate and Banton for drugs and firearms offences. Elsewhere, the music is often characterised by its 'slackness', depressingly formulaic, lurid and sexist lyrics and dance routines.

It doesn't have to be like this of course and isn't always. Banton made his name with the truly toxic and inflammatory anti-gay Boom Bye Bye, but before his incarceration he had gone on to make an excellent roots album Til Shiloh. One of its stand out tracks is entitled Murderer. In an echo of the previous era, it has become an anthem of many protests against deaths in custody in the decades that have followed.

As these words were being written artists such as Third World, Misty and Mykal Rose were keeping the flame of conscious reggae alive. Marley's oldest son Ziggy and Damian the only child born of his relationship with Cindy Breakspeare have gone on to make some creditable albums, notably the latter's Welcome to Jamrock which skilfully samples some of his father's work. He has recorded material with various artists including the American rapper Nas and become a respected and renowned producer.

One month before he died Marley was awarded the Order of Merit, Jamaica's highest honour by Seaga. Following his death a series of commemorative stamps using the titles of many of his most famous songs and images from various albums were issued by the Jamaican postal service. The speed with which he was appropriated by the powerful and privileged was quite breathtaking.

Glorious failure?

Arguably, Marley's career, exemplified by both the Smile Jamaica and One Love concerts and the Zimbabwe debacle could be characterised as a glorious failure. For one thing, certainly in the United States he never quite reached the audience he hoped to attract. Whilst he was revered by the likes of *Rolling Stone* (the magazine was as keen as the band) and white college students, he was never fully embraced by black Americans. Invariably the crowd at most Wailers gigs was overwhelmingly white. Moreover, Bradley suggests that Bob's portrait is frequently found on living room walls alongside that of other great black heroes, such as King, Malcolm and Rosa Parks. Flick through the occupant's record collection however and one will struggle to find a copy of any of his albums.

More importantly the emancipation that Bob dedicated his life to proclaiming could never be achieved through adherence to Rastafarianism. The uncomfortable truth about Selassie's mortality and shortcomings is one factor but not the only one. The reality is that Rastafarianism is ultimately a mass of unrealistic aspirations.

On one level the Marxist critique of religion that we considered earlier does not seem to quite fit at least not if we apply it to Marley's interpretation of the faith. The characterisation is invariably used to criticise those who eschew struggle in the belief that something better awaits them in the afterlife. But as we can see from many of his most famous lyrics, song and album titles, Uprising', Wake Up and Live and, perhaps most obviously, Revolution, Marley didn't simply believe in blind faith. His Rastafarianism did involve a call to arms. So too seemingly did that of Tosh. He is often regarded as having been the most militant of the Wailers and his most famous lyrical composition Get Up, Stand Up apparently needs no explanation.

And yet when we do study it, we realise that its words really do highlight the contradiction at the heart of the philosophy. It begins:

Get up, stand up
Stand up for your rights
Get up, stand up
Don't give up the fight

So far so militant and its denunciation of more orthodox religions could not be more emphatic:

Preacherman don't tell me heaven is under the earth
I know you don't know
What life is really worth

And it dismisses the idea of 'Dyin' and goin' to heaven in Jesus name'.

The song then goes on to assert however that 'We're sick and tired of your 'ism, schism game'. The reference to 'isms' is an explicit rejection of political philosophies including capitalism, socialism and communism. This is perhaps understandable given the horrors that were being revealed both by the rampant capitalism of the US led western world and the supposed communism of the bloc controlled by the Soviet Union. As we have noted, despite its size, Jamaica was both economically and strategically important enough to be drawn into the Cold War.

Unfortunately however, whilst he was right to denounce the inequities of the 'shitstem' Tosh's own 'ism' does not offer a clear or coherent alternative.

Get Up, Stand Up concludes:

If you know what life is worth.
You will look for your's on earth
So now you see the light
Stand up for your rights.

What exactly does this mean? On the one hand it seems to be a defiant demand for self-activity but on the other, as we know, the god on earth that Rastafarians looked to was Selassie. Listen to, the final 'Stand up for your rights' on the studio version and what you hear is a triumphant 'Jah!'

Similarly, if we examine that last, great poignant statement from Marley, Redemption Song, it begins with a denunciation of slavery but then an immediate declaration that his hand is 'made strong by the hand of The Almighty'. He then proceeds to cite Garvey's words. Here the suggestion seems to be that we can be the agents of our own liberation. But we are then told to 'Have no fear for atomic energy cause none of them can stop the time'. This apparent reference to the proliferation of nuclear weapons which was a signal feature of the Cold War is surely, profoundly mistaken.

He then asserts:

> *How long shall they kill our prophets*
> *While we stand aside and look*
> *Some say it's just a part of it*
> *We've got to fulfil the Book*

We are urged to respond and do something, but it is in order to fulfil a pre-ordained plan. The sufferers are not the real authors of their own destiny therefore. Their only real task is to answer the call to complete the journey to Zion.

In reality Rastafarianism represented a recipe for retreat, passivity and a reliance on somebody else, Jah, sitting atop Mount Zion to 'rule all creation'.[61] To return to Marx then, in a very real sense it was an opium of the people. Very few of its followers were really intent on making the journey to Ethiopia. Instead they remained in Jamaica, London, Birmingham or wherever, smoking spliff and chanting down Babylon. This perhaps explains why theorists such as C.L.R. James could acknowledge the anti-colonial sentiments, but nevertheless remained somewhat lukewarm towards roots reggae and and sceptical about Rastafarianism.

One Love

None of this should diminish our admiration of Marley and neither should the cynical appropriation of him by the Establishment. Regardless of the wealth he amassed, he never forgot his roots. He remained a man of the people and although he sometimes went away, it was to them that he always returned. He was a champion of the marginalised and oppressed and as such, he is an inspiration to us all.

Yes, he was devoutly religious and expressed his hopes and aspirations in spiritual terms. The plain truth is though that like his two great predecessors Malcolm X and Martin Luther King, and unlike those Rastafarians who retreated to the mountains, he was both religious and a man of action; someone who identified with the 'real revolutionaries'. He didn't simply ask us to have faith. Instead he encouraged us to 'stand up and fight.' It is fitting that he was buried with both his Bible and the 'axe' that was his weapon of choice, his red Gibson Les Paul guitar. Evidently Rita also popped a little stalk of ganja into the coffin to send him on his way in style!

Yes, he espoused views that seemed to mark him out as a black separatist. But to pigeonhole him too narrowly would be to do him a disservice. He was understandably troubled by his ancestry and it fuelled his militancy but ultimately when pressed he declared:

> Me don't' deh pon nobody's side. Me don't deh pon de black man's side. Nor pon de white man's side. Me deh pon God's side.

We began this little book with a reference to the Marley album that has sold the highest number, Legend and the one that has won the most plaudits, Exodus. Two tracks that appear on both those releases that I was determined not to mention are One

Love/People Get Ready and Three Little Birds. This was not simply because I don't like the plodding, pedestrian tunes. I don't like the lyrics either. I simply don't believe that we should 'give thanks and praise to the Lord' or that we shouldn't 'worry about a thing' because 'every little thing's gonna be alright.' I have always thought that these two songs were deliberately promoted to downplay Marley's militancy and instead showcase a happy, contented and harmless Rasta.

On reflection however there is something to be said about his evocation of the simple pleasures of life in Three Little Birds. As I forced myself to listen to it again, it reminded me of the Russian revolutionary Leon Trotsky's own last testament, written in 1940 during the very darkest of times. The great revolution he had led had been destroyed, the world was in turmoil and he was living in exile. Yet he still had faith in the potential of human beings to make the world a better place and could declare that through the window:

> I can see the bright green strip of grass beneath the wall, and the clear blue sky above the wall, and sunlight everywhere. Life is beautiful. Let the future generations cleanse it of all evil, oppression and violence, and enjoy it to the full.[62]

Man of faith, militant, Pan-Africanist, Marley was all of those things. Above all, he really did believe in 'one love'. Fittingly Macdonald's documentary concludes with Bob's own spoken words. They are emblazoned across the screen but really need no translation:

> I don't really have no ambition you know. I only really have one thing I'd really like to see happen. I'd like to see mankind live together. Black, white, Chinese everyone. You know what I mean? That's all.[63]

Notes

1 Barrett Sr, Leonard E: *The Rastafarians: Twentieth Anniversary Edition*, Beacon Press, Boston 1997. p1

2 Akwei A, 'Another Strongman for Ethiopia' *Human Rights Watch Now Blog* 22 August 2012 *http://blog.amnestyusa.org/africa/another-strongman-for-ethiopia/*

3 Barrett op cit p29

4 James, C.L.R. (written under his pseudonymn J R Johnson) 'Revolution and The Negro', *New International* Vol V, December 1939 *https://www.marxists.org/archive/james-clr/works/1939/12/negro-revolution.htm*

5 James, C.L.R., 'The Making of the Caribbean People', in *Spheres of Existence: Selected Writings, Vol. 2* (Allison and Busby, 1980), p177.

6 Barrett, ibid pp 34-35

7 Blackburn, Robin, *The Overthrow of Colonial Slavery, 1776-1848* (London: Verso, 2011), p55.

8 Blackburn, ibid, p432.

9 The beneficiares included General Sir James Duff, an army officer and sometime MP for Banffshire who received £4,101, the equivalent of £3 million today. One of Duff's ancestors is none other than the Rt Hon David Cameron. As this book was being completed, the British Prime Minister was embarking upon a trip to Jamaica during which he happily announced the provision of funding to build a new prison, but sidestepped demands for reparations to atone for slavery.

10 cited in Morley Jonathan The Morant Bay Rebellion BBC Coventry & Warwickshire *http://bbc.co.uk/coventry/content/articles/2007/03/28/morant_bay_rebellion_feature.shtml?page=1*

11 For more on Morant Bay, see Heuman, Gad, *'The Killing Time': The Morant Bay Rebellion in Jamaica* (Knoxville: University of Tennessee Press, 1994).

12 *Jamaica Gleaner* 2nd May 1938 reported in Hart, Richard, *Labour Rebellions of the 1930s in the British Caribbean Regional Colonies* (London: Socialist History Society, 2002), online at *http://www.socialisthistorysociety.co.uk/HART.HTM*

13 The History of the JLP *http://www.jamaicalabourparty.com/content/history-jlp*

14 Bradley Lloyd, *Bass Culture*, Viking 2000, p14

15 Crazy Baldheads from Rastaman Vibration, 1976 album

16 Article in *The Blackman*, 8th November 1930 *http://www. africaresource.com/rasta/sesotris-the-great-the-egyptian-hercules/ the-prophesy-by-marcus-garvey/*

17 Marx Karl, *A Contribution to the Critique of Hegel's Philosophy of Right – 1844*

18 *http://daghettotymz.com/current/selassie/selassie.html*

19 *Jamaica Gleaner* 'Rastas mark 50th anniversary of bloody Coral Gardens incident' – 3rd April 2013 *http://www.jamaicaobserver.com/ news/Rasatas-mark-50th-anniversary-of-bloody-Coral-Gardens-incident_13976856*

20 Barrett op cit.p2

21 See for example Kevin Anderson's excellent 2012 documentary *Marley*

22 First broadcast on Radio 1 in 1982 and again in 1983, Linton Kwesi Johnson's *From Mento to Lovers Rock* was given a fresh airing on BBC Radio 6 Music in the summer of 2015

23 Bradley Lloyd, *Bass Culture*, Viking 2000

24 Bradley, ibid p11

25 Bradley, ibid p49

26 Dodd and others were in the habit of scratching off the names of the artists and the song titles so that there rivals could not identify the original songs and then giving them names of their own associated with their soundsystem.

27 Bradley, ibid p84

28 Linton Kwesi Johnson, *From Mento to Lovers Rock*

29 Bradley, op cit p162

30 Bradley, ibid pp174-175

31 Dandy Livingstone A Message to You Rudy, Trojan 1967

32 Prince Buster Judge Dread Bluebeat Records (1967)

33 Bradley op cit p199

34 Bradley, ibid p342

35 Bradley ibid p42

36 White Timothy *'Chris Blackwell – An Interview with the Founding Father of the Reggae Music Industry'* in Bordowitz op cit. p266

37 The Bible – Matthew 3:10 (New Testament)

> *And now also the axe is laid*
> *unto the root of the trees:*
> *therefore every tree which*
> *bringeth not forth good fruit is*
> *hewn down, and cast into the fire.*

38 Unlikely though it is, it would be nice to think that Marley drew his inspiration for this metaphor from the great Russian revolutionary Leon Trotsky, who in 1936, writing about the importance of theoretical clarity for any revolutionary organisation, stressed that 'A small axe can fell a large tree only if is sharp enough'. Trotsky, Leon, 'Once Again: The ILP – An Interview', *New International* Vol 3 No.1, February 1936 *https://www.marxists.org/archive/trotsky/1936/xx/ilp.htm* Clearly great minds do think alike.

39 This episode is recalled by Manley in Bodowitz H (ed.) *Every Little Thing Gonna be Alright – Bob Marley Reader* Da Capo Press Cambridge MA 2004 p222

40 Macdonald Kevin, Marley Shangri-La and Tuff Gong Pictures in association with Cowboy Films 2012

41 James, Marlon, *A Brief History of Seven Killings*, Riverhead Books 2014

42 She uses this term when asked on camera about Bob's affairs when interviewed for the film Marley.

43 Marley Rita, *No Woman , No Cry: My Life With Bob Marley*, Sidgwick & Jackson 2004 p142

44 Ibid p142

45 White, op cit p301

46 Bob Marley in Zimbabwe: The Untold Story. adapted by Ree Ngwenya from Bob Marley Songs of Freedom by Adrian Boot and Chris Salewicz in *The Bob Marley Reader*. op cit p228

47 'Ism, skism' is a phrase which appears elsewhere notably in Get Up, Stand Up, penned by Peter Tosh. 'Ism' refers to belief systems. Skism is a reference to the divisions (schisms) that these ideologies led to.

48 London is the Place For Me – Lord Kitchener, Honest Jon's Records 2003

49 Dresser, Madge, *Black and White on the Buses: The 1963 Colour Bar Dispute in Bristol* (Bookmarks 2013)

50 See 'Claudia Jones: Fighting For Multiculturalism from below' in Hassan Mahamdallie, *Black British Rebels: Figures From Working Class History* (Bookmarks) 2012

51 First published by the Caribbean Educational and Community Workers Association and New Beacon Books, it was reprinted as part of Brian Richardson(ed.) *Tell It Like It Is: How Our Schools Fail Black Children*, Bookmarks & Trentham Books (2007)

52 James, C.L.R. 'The West Indies – microcosm: Interviewed by Paul Buhle and Jim Murray', in Paul Buhle, Jayne Cortez, Philip Lamantia, Nancy Joyce Peters, Franklin Rosemont and Penelope Rosemont (eds.) *Free Spirits: Annals of the Insurgent Imagination* (City Lights Books, San Francisco, 1982), p91.

53 In an interview for the November issue of *Uncut* magazine

54 Cited in Richardson B (ed.) *Say it Loud – Marxism and the Fight Against Racism* – Bookmarks, London 2013 p89

55 Not to be confused with Junior Marvin, The Wailers guitarist

56 Gilroy, Paul. *There Ain't No Black in the Union Jack.* (Routledge, London) 2002 p161

57 Jah Pickney (RAR) from Tribute to the Martyrs – Steel Pulse (Island Records 1979)

58 Itself an original language rude boy classic starring Jimmy Cliff

59 African Children – Aswad from the album New Chapter (CBS 1981)

60 Ghost Town – The Specials (2 Tone, 1981)

61 Marley's words from Exodus

62 Lovell, Sarak, ed Leon Trotsky Speaks, New York 1972 cited in Cliff, Tony, *The Darker the NIght the Brighter the Star: Trotsky, 1927-1940* London Bookmarks 1993 pp 380-81

63 Anderson – Marley op cit 2012

Appendicies

i   *Bob Marley selected discography*

According to his official website, there are currently 42 Bob Marley & The Wailers albums that have been released during his lifetime or in the decades since. Listed below is a selection that includes the main studio releases, the great 1975 Live album and the best selling compilation Legend.

The Wailing Wailers	(Studio One, 1965)
Soul Rebels	(Trojan, 1970)
Soul Revolution Part 2	(Upsetter, 1971)
Best of The Wailers	(Beverley, 1971)
Catch A Fire	(Island, 1973)
Burnin'	(Island, 1973)
Natty Dread	(Island, 1974)
Live	(Island, 1975)
Rastaman Vibration	(Island, 1976)
Exodus	(Island, 1977)
Kaya	(Island, 1978)
Survival	(Island, 1979)
Uprising	(Island, 1980)
Confrontation	(Island, 1983)
Legend	(Island, 1984)

Fighting fascism today

The demise of the NF in the early 1980s did not of course bring an end to racism in Britain. Anyone who thought it might do would receive a rude awakening. In 1978 the then Leader of the Opposition Margaret Thatcher gave an infamous interview during which she declared and sympathised with the idea that 'People are really rather afraid that this country might be rather swamped by people of a different culture'.

This was an ominous indication that state racism that would persist under her government. Institutional racism continued and was only finally recognised by the authorities in 1999 as a result of the Stephen Lawrence Family Campaign's heroic fight for justice.

The defeat and demise of the NF did however help to create a climate in which multiculturalism and anti-racism flourished. The 1980s and early 90s was a period when, in the words of anti-racist writer and activist Darcus Howe, youngsters could grow up "black and at ease" less concerned about racist violence. It was also a period when our prospects of going to university and getting better jobs improved.

We can never afford to be complacent however. We had to continue fighting racism throughout that period and it was only a matter of time before the Fascists re-grouped. By the beginning of the 1990s there was an alarming increase in Fascist violence and it was in these circumstances that the Anti Nazi League (ANL) was reformed to counter the growth of the British National Party (BNP), the successor organisation to the NF.

Since 2003 this struggle has been taken forward by Unite Against Fascism, (UAF). In the past dozen years UAF has played a critical role in driving the BNP from the political mainstream to the margins and stopping the fascist English Defence League (EDL) in its tracks. It is also at the forefront of trying to build a European wide movement against the alarming rise of fascism on the continent.

Love Music Hate Racism (LMHR) was set up in 2002, also in response to rising levels of racism and electoral successes for the BNP. Like RAR before it, LMHR uses the energy of the music scene to celebrate diversity and involve people in anti-racist and anti-fascist activity as well as to urge people to vote against fascist candidates in elections. LMHR has helped to mobilise against further BNP election victories and the activities of the EDL.

Further information including how to join and get involved in UAF and LMHR activities can be found at:

www.uaf.org.uk

http://lovemusichateracism.com

Steel Pulse *playing Klu-Klux-Klan at the RAR/ANL Carnival, Victoria Park London 1978*

In June 2014 *Mojo* magazine published a list compiled by its staff of the 50 greatest reggae albums. Musical preferences are such a personal choice that these things are always fraught with danger. Catch A Fire comes out on top of the magazine's pile but Exodus doesn't make the Top 10 and no other Marley album is included in the chart at all. I would want to include Marley's entire catalogue of Island studio recordings as well as the 1975 recording of the great Lyceum gig. The Live album would surely be worth including for the wonderful version of No Woman, No Cry alone let alone the other fantastic stuff. Elsewhere Handsworth Revolution is a great album but if I was choosing just one Steel Pulse record I would pick either True Democracy or Tribute to the Martyrs. The latter includes the brilliant Jah Pickney - Rock Against Racism. Nevertheless the *Mojo* list provides a pretty comprehensive sweep of the history of the genre and can be found at *www.mojo4music.com/15098/50-greatest-reggae-albums.com*

I've selected just 20 of the albums in the Mojo list, excluding Marley's work and have restricted my list to one per artist. In alphabetical order they are:

Aswad	New Chapter	*CBS*
Augustus Pablo	King Tubby Meets Rockers	*Rockers*
Big Youth	Screaming Target	*Trojan*
Black Uhuru	Anthem	*Mango*
Bunny Wailer	Blackheart Man	*Island*
Burning Spear	Marcus Garvey	*Island*
Culture	Two Sevens Clash	*Lightning*
Don Drummond	Best of	*Studio One*
Gregory Isaacs	Night Nurse	*Island*
Lee 'Scratch' Perry & The Upsetters	Super Ape	*Mango*
Marcia Griffiths	Naturally	*Sky Note*
Mikey Dread	World War III	*Dread at the Controls*
Peter Tosh	Legalize It	*Virgin*
Prince Buster	Fabulous (Greatest Hits)	*Melodic*
The Skatalites	Ska-Boo-Da-Ba	*Top Deck*
Steel Pulse	Handsworth Revolution	*Island*
Toots & the Maytals	Funky Kingston	*Mango*
U Roy	Version Galore	*Treasure Island*
Various	Club Ska '67	*WIRL*
Various	The Harder They Come	*Island*

In addition my own additions would include:

The Beat	Complete Beat	*Shout! Factory*
Misty in Roots	John Peel Sessions	*BBC*
The Selecter	Too Much Pressure	*Two Tone*
The Specials	Best Of	*EMI 2008*
Third World	96 Degrees in the Shade	*Island*
UB40	Signing Off	*Graduate*

Of course **The Clash** were not strictly speaking a reggae band but they were such an important feature of RAR that it would be remiss of me not to include them, so London Calling (CBS,1979) makes my list as well. 26 is a strange number to finish on so 4 more to bring us up to a round 30 are:

Damian Marley	Welcome to Jamrock	*Tuff Gong*
Desmond Dekker	007 The Best of	*Trojan*
Jimmy Cliff	Wonderful World, Beautiful People	
		A&M
Linton Kwesi Johnson		
	Bass Culture	*Island*

+ additions from **Redwords**

Jackie Mittoo	The Keyboard King	*Universal Sound*
Don Letts (DJ mix)	Dread Meets Punk Rockers Uptown	
		Heavenly
The Front Line	Reggae Classics *(3CDs)*	*EMI France 2008*

The current period has seen the rise of Islamophobia, a resurgence of fascism in Europe and constant attempts to scapegoat immigrants. This book seeks to challenge the idea that racism is inevitable by taking a critical look at the origins and history of racism in Britain and abroad. It looks in particular at the experience of the last 40 years in Britain, from the struggles of the 1970s through the 1981 riots, Stephen Lawrence and the war on terror. Highlighting key examples of black and white unity, resistance and struggle in the US and Britain, it intervenes in current debates about racism and sets out the Marxist case for how best to fight it. The eight authors shared Marxist approach and activist history ensure a smooth narrative and a clear argument for the struggle for liberation today.

Edited by
Brian Richardson
£7.50

ISBN : 978 1 909026 38 4

Say It Loud:
Marxism and the
Fight Against the
Racism

Mariner, Renegade & Castaway:
Chris Braithwaite
Seamen's Organiser, Socialist and Militant Pan-Africanist

CHRISTIAN HØGSBJERG

Chris Braithwaite (aka 'Chris Jones') was a black Barbadian seaman who became a leading organiser of colonial seamen in inter-war Britain. He played a critical role in the Pan-Africanist and wider anti-colonial movement alongside figures such as C L R James and George Padmore. Christian Høgsbjerg recovers Braithwaite's long overlooked life as a black radical and political trade unionist, and suggests his determined struggle for working class unity in the face of racism and austerity retains relevance for us today.

'Through his scrupulous research of the compelling life and times of Chris Braithwaite, Christian Høgsbjerg has uncovered the vital contribution of a pioneering black activist and anti-colonial stalwart. Braithwaite's brave achievement should be on the curriculum of all our schools.' – Chris Searle, Race and Class

'Høgsbjerg shines light on a generation of radical fighters against racism and exploitation, caught between the spark of light generated by the 1917 Bolshevik revolution and the crushing darkness of Stalinism.' – *Hassan Mahamdallie,* author Black British Rebels

£4.00

ISBN: 978 1 909026 56 8
socialisthistorysociety.co.uk
redwords.org.uk
bookmarksbookshop.co.uk

1 Bloomsbury Street, London WC1B 3QE

REDWORDS